Inner Child Recovery Workbook

Healing Your Inner Child from Childhood
Trauma, Abandonment, and Abuse to
Find Peace and Happiness

VitalSpark Synergy

Table of Contents

INTRODUCTION.. 3

The Importance of Healing 4

PART 1: RECOGNIZING THE WOUNDED INNER CHILD 7

IDENTIFYING THE SIGNS 9

Exercise: Self-Assessment Checklist 10

Doing the Work... 13

ORIGINS OF PAIN 15

Mapping Personal History 18

ACKNOWLEDGMENT 25

Activity: Guided Reflection Prompts 27

PART 2: TECHNIQUES FOR HEALING 33

COMMUNICATION WITH THE INNER CHILD..................................... 35

Exercise: Inner Child Dialogue... 37

Exercise: Mirror Work 40

REPARENTING THE SELF 43

Exercise 1: Creating Your Reparenting Plan............................ 46

Exercise 2: Inner Child Date 48

Exercise 3: Reparenting Through Visualization 51

EMOTIONAL PROCESSING.. 55

Exercise: Emotional Release Through Letter Writing.............. 58

Guided Imagery Exercise: The Healing Pool............................ 61

PART 3: TRANSFORMING THE SELF...67

CHANGING THE NARRATIVE 69

Exercise: Dialogue With Your Inner Critic 71

Activity: Crafting New Affirmations and Narratives 74

BUILDING NEW BELIEFS 79

Worksheet: Belief Restructuring Exercises............................. 83

DEVELOPING EMOTIONAL RESILIENCE.. 89

30-Day Emotional Resilience Challenge.................................. 92

PART 4: INTEGRATION AND FREEDOM 97

ADVANCES IN NEUROSCIENCE: EMPOWERING INNER CHILD HEALING 99

Mirror Neuron Empathy Exercise... 100

Exercise: Rewiring the Brain for Safety and Connection........... 103

PREVENTING THE REINFORCEMENT OF INNER WOUNDS 107

    Inner Child Advocate Roleplay 108

    Prevention Plan Exercise 111

INTEGRATING THE INNER CHILD 117

    Integration Visualization Exercise 118

    Embodied Inner Child Play 119

    Maintaining Emotional Health 121

    Monthly Emotional Health Maintenance Checklist 125

    Emotional Health Vision Board 127

LIVING FREELY 131

    Exercise: Gratitude Storytelling 132

CONCLUSION **139**

REFERENCES **143**

SPECIAL BONUS!

Want this Bonus book for Free?

Get FREE, unlimited access to it and all my new books by joining the Fan Base!

Introduction

Imagine for a moment the child you once were. Picture that innocent, wide-eyed little one—so full of wonder, trust, and potential. That child still lives within you today, carrying the echoes of your earliest experiences, both joyful and painful.

For many of us, that inner child bears wounds—scars from traumas, unmet needs, or moments when we felt unworthy or unloved. We may not think about that little one often, but their heartaches continue to shape us beneath the surface, influencing how we see ourselves, relate to others, and experience the world as adults.

Our younger selves can get stuck in time, holding tight to the painful stories and beliefs we absorbed in our most formative years. An unhealed inner child can manifest in many ways: a deep sense of emptiness, a harsh inner critic, struggles with self-worth, unsatisfying relationships. Patterns that once protected that vulnerable child can harden into armor that keeps us disconnected from our authentic selves and others.

These wounds often trace back to our earliest relationships with caregivers. Even in the most loving families, no parent is perfect. There are inevitable moments of misattunement, times when that developing child doesn't get the mirroring, validation, or consistent loving presence they need. For some, the wounds are deeper—abuse, neglect, addiction in the household, or the loss of a parent. The child makes sense of their world the best they can, but often takes on the blame, believing they are somehow fundamentally flawed or unlovable.

As we grow, we unconsciously internalize the voices of our caregivers. The messages we received, whether spoken or unspoken, become our inner dialogue. "You're too much." "You're not enough." "It's not okay to feel." We learn to exile parts of ourselves to be accepted and loved. We build our identity around these fractured pieces, not realizing how much we've walled off our true essence.

But here's the hopeful truth: By courageously revisiting those tender places with curiosity and compassion, we can heal. We all have the capacity to re-parent ourselves, to offer our inner child the loving attunement they always needed. In doing so, we don't just soothe old heartaches; we open the door to profound transformation—a homecoming to wholeness.

This is deep soul work. It requires courage to venture into the shadowy corners of our psyche, to sit with the ache we've long avoided. It takes patience and persistence to untangle old narratives and forge new neural pathways. But with the right road map and supportive tools, we can alchemize pain into resilience, self-compassion, and authentic joy.

The Importance of Healing

Embarking on inner child recovery work is one of the most profound gifts we can give ourselves. It's an act of radical self-love that ripples outward, shifting how we show up in our relationships and in the world.

When we validate our inner child's pains and unmet needs, we reclaim lost parts of ourselves. We widen our window of tolerance for discomfort and develop resilience. We learn to set healthy boundaries, communicate bravely, and be authentic. This inner attunement becomes a renewable wellspring of self-compassion and groundedness.

As we heal, we start to release the armor we've carried. We develop more intimate, fulfilling connections. Instead of being easily triggered into old shame spirals or lashing out in defensiveness, we respond from a place of rooted self-worth. We advocate for our needs with clarity and compassion. We attract partners and friends who honor our wholeness.

Beyond personal relationships, this work empowers us to dream bigger. We start to dismantle limiting beliefs about what we're capable of. We take risks, embrace creativity, and step into leadership in new ways. When we know we can meet our own needs, we're less attached to external validation and more free to boldly pursue our passions.

Most importantly, inner child recovery allows us to extend grace to ourselves and others. We more clearly see the wounded child in those around us. We hold space for loved ones' healing without taking on the burden as our own. We model vulnerability and emotional intelligence for our children, helping to break generational cycles.

Ultimately, this deep work allows us to author a new story—one where we know our inherent worth, regardless of our past. We release old shame and limiting beliefs. We trust ourselves more. We take up space unapologetically. We let love in. This is the path of wholeness—integrating all the parts of ourselves with honesty and grace.

If you've picked up this book, know that you're brave. Know that you're worth the effort. And know that you're not alone on this path. With the right tools and supportive guidance, you can help your inner child feel seen, soothed, and safe. You can regain that childlike sense of wonder and potential. Your future self is already cheering you on.

Part 1:

Recognizing the Wounded Inner

Child

Let's dive into the first part of our journey: recognizing the signs of a wounded inner child. This is where we start to get curious about the patterns and behaviors that may be holding us back from wholehearted living.

Take a deep breath, and let's approach this with compassion. We're not here to judge or blame but to shine a light of understanding. We'll explore some common symptoms, do a little self-assessment, and even map out the origins of our pain.

This process may feel uncomfortable at times, as we're uncovering parts of ourselves that we may have kept hidden for years, even decades. But remember, discomfort is often a sign that we're growing, that we're stepping into new territory. And in this case, that new territory is a deeper understanding and acceptance of ourselves.

It's crucial to remember that we're not alone. Countless others have walked this path before us, and countless more will follow. By bravely facing our own wounds, we're not only healing ourselves but also contributing to the collective healing of humanity.

Remember, this isn't about wallowing in the past but acknowledging our experiences so we can heal in the present. It's a brave thing you're doing, and I'm honored to be on this path with you.

So, grab your favorite cozy beverage, find a quiet spot, and let's start peeling back the layers. Your inner child is ready to be seen and heard.

Trust the process, and know that every step, however small, is a step toward wholeness.

You've got this. Let's do it together.

Identifying the Signs

Alright, friends. We're diving in. We're starting this journey of inner child healing by getting real about how those old wounds show up in our day-to-day lives. Because here's the thing: Those hurts we experienced as kids? They don't just magically disappear. They linger, often in sneaky ways that we might not even fully recognize.

So, let's talk about some of the common signs that your inner child might be in need of some TLC. Do you find yourself constantly seeking approval, morphing yourself to make others happy? Do you struggle with trusting people, always waiting for the other shoe to drop? Are you your own worst critic, quick to beat yourself up over the smallest mistake?

While these behaviors might feel familiar and even strangely comforting, they are often strategies we developed as kids to cope with pain or to feel safe and loved. They served a purpose then, but as adults, they can keep us feeling stuck and disconnected from our authentic selves.

And it's not just our relationship with ourselves that can be impacted. Our inner child wounds often play out in our interactions with others, too. We might find ourselves drawn to partners who mirror the inconsistent love we received growing up. Or, we might keep even our closest loved ones at arm's length, terrified of vulnerability.

Now, I know this might feel heavy. You might be tempted to slip into shame, to berate yourself for not having it all figured out. But can we just take a collective deep breath and remember that we're all works in progress? These patterns are not character flaws. They're understandable adaptations to the challenges we faced as kids.

Let's approach this with curiosity and compassion. I've included a self-assessment checklist to help you identify some of your unique symptoms. As you go through it, try to channel your inner researcher. Observe your behaviors and thoughts with interest, not judgment.

Remember, naming these patterns is not about blame. It's about shining a light so we can start to make shifts. It's about extending grace to ourselves and honoring the journey.

And trust me, I know this work isn't easy. It takes courage to look at our pain and acknowledge how we've been shaped by it. But you're here, and that tells me you've got that brave, badass spirit within you.

Take your time with this. Be patient with yourself. Know that every moment of self-awareness is a step toward healing. You're doing sacred work, my friend. And I'm cheering you on every step of the way.

Let's keep going, together.

Exercise: Self-Assessment Checklist

Let's look into this self-assessment with open hearts and curious minds. Remember, this is a journey of self-discovery, not self-judgment. Take a deep breath, grab your favorite journal or a piece of paper, and let's get started.

Step 1: Set the Stage: Find a quiet, comfortable space where you feel safe and won't be disturbed. Light a candle, brew a cup of tea, or put on some soothing music if that feels good to you. Create a little sanctuary for yourself.

Step 2: Connect With Your Inner Child: Close your eyes and take a few deep breaths. Place one hand on your heart and one on your belly. Imagine your inner child—that younger version of yourself that experienced pain or unmet needs. Visualize them in as much detail as you can. What are they wearing? What's the expression on their face? Send them a message of love and reassurance. Let them know that you're here now, ready to listen and honor their experiences.

Step 3: Review the Statements: Now, open your eyes and read through the following statements. For each one, take a moment to check in with yourself. Does this resonate with your experience? If so, make a mark next to it in your journal. Remember, there are no right or wrong answers. This is about your truth.

1. I often feel like an imposter, afraid that others will see me as inadequate or unworthy.

2. I have a hard time asserting my needs and desires, often putting others' wants before my own.

3. I'm highly self-critical and quick to blame myself when things go wrong.

4. I tend to be a people-pleaser, morphing myself to gain others' approval.

5. I struggle with trusting others, always expecting to be let down or abandoned.

6. I have a hard time fully relaxing and letting my guard down, even with loved ones.

7. I often feel a sense of emptiness or emotional numbness.

8. I'm uncomfortable with conflict and will go to great lengths to avoid it.

9. I have a deep fear of rejection and will do anything to avoid it.

10. I often feel guilty or ashamed for having needs or expressing emotions.

11. I have a hard time setting and maintaining healthy boundaries.

12. I often feel like a child in adult relationships, seeking constant reassurance.

13. I have a history of unfulfilling or even abusive relationships.

14. I tend to be either overly responsible or irresponsible in my daily life.

15. I struggle with addiction or compulsive behaviors.

16. I often feel anxious, depressed, or easily overwhelmed.

17. I have a hard time accessing or expressing anger in a healthy way.

18. I tend to be overly rigid and controlling or excessively laid-back and unstructured.

19. I often feel unheard or invisible in social situations.

20. I have a deep sense that something is wrong with me.

Step 4: Reflect and Journal: Look over the statements you marked. Take a few deep breaths, and then start writing. Let your thoughts and feelings flow onto the page without censorship. What comes up for you as you read these statements? What memories or experiences do they evoke? What patterns do you notice?

Remember, this isn't about crafting perfect prose. It's about letting your inner child speak and about validating their experiences.

Step 5: Offer Compassion: Once you've finished writing, take a moment to re-read what you've written. Then, imagine saying these words to your inner child. What would you say to comfort them, to reassure them? Write a letter to your inner child, offering them the compassion, validation, and love they needed then and still need now.

Step 6: Close With Care: When you feel ready, close your journal. Take a few more deep breaths, wiggle your fingers and toes, and gently bring your awareness back to the present moment. Thank your inner child for their bravery in sharing with you. Promise them that you'll keep showing up, that you're in this healing journey together.

And finally, do something kind for yourself. Stretch, dance, have a nourishing meal, call a friend—whatever feels like an act of self-love. Remember, you're doing profound, courageous work. Be gentle with yourself.

Doing the Work

As we close this chapter on recognizing the signs of a wounded inner child, I want to take a moment to honor you. Yes, you. You, who have courageously chosen to embark on this journey of healing. You, who have dared to look at your pain with eyes of compassion. You are the one who is taking the first steps toward reclaiming your wholeness.

I know this work isn't easy. Facing our wounds and acknowledging how they have shaped us takes immense strength. It takes a willingness to be vulnerable and to sit with discomfort. And yet, here you are, showing up for yourself in the most profound way.

Remember, identifying these patterns and behaviors is not about self-blame or shame. It's about understanding, about extending grace to ourselves. It's about recognizing that our coping strategies, while they may have served us in the past, might not be serving us anymore.

This is the beginning of a new chapter. By shining a light on these wounds, you're creating space for healing. You're opening the door to new ways of being, more fulfilling relationships, and a deeper connection with your authentic self.

As you move forward, keep nurturing that relationship with your inner child. Keep listening to their needs and validating their experiences. Keep showing up for them with love and patience.

And trust the process. Healing is not linear. There will be ups and downs, breakthroughs and setbacks. But every moment of self-awareness, every act of self-compassion, is planting seeds of transformation.

You're not alone on this path. In the coming chapters, we'll dive deeper into the origins of these wounds and explore practical strategies for healing. But for now, take a moment to celebrate how far you've already come.

Origins of Pain

Welcome back, brave soul. In the last chapter, we began to identify the signs of a wounded inner child—those patterns and behaviors that may be holding us back from living wholeheartedly. Today, we're going to dive deeper to explore the origins of these wounds.

Because here's the thing: Our pain has roots. Those coping strategies we developed, those beliefs we hold about ourselves and the world, they didn't emerge from nowhere. They were shaped by our experiences, especially those early, formative experiences.

I remember a moment from my childhood that illustrates this perfectly. I was about 6 years old, excitedly telling a story to my family at the dinner table. In my enthusiasm, I knocked over my glass of milk. Instead of being met with understanding, I was scolded harshly and told that I was "too much," "too clumsy," and "too loud." That moment, seemingly small in the grand scheme of things, left an imprint. It taught me that my exuberance was problematic and that I needed to shrink myself to be loved.

This is just one example, but it highlights how the wounds we carry often have their origins in these everyday interactions and experiences. And while it's easy to dismiss these moments as insignificant, the truth is that they are profoundly impactful to a child's developing brain and sense of self.

Unfortunately, our society often minimizes or dismisses childhood emotional pain. We're told to "get over it," that "sticks and stones may break my bones, but words will never hurt me." But the reality is that emotional wounds can be just as painful and long-lasting as physical ones. And when we deny or invalidate these experiences, we only deepen the harm.

So, let's talk about some of the common sources of inner child wounds. First, there's trauma. And when we say trauma, we often think of the big, life-altering events—abuse, violence, the loss of a parent. And yes, those experiences certainly leave a profound impact. Studies have consistently shown that childhood trauma is linked to a wide range of mental and physical health challenges in adulthood, from depression and anxiety to chronic pain and autoimmune disorders.

But trauma can also be more subtle, more insidious. It can be the constant tension in a household rife with addiction or mental illness. It can be the accumulated impact of being bullied or ostracized at school. It can be the medical procedure that, while necessary, left us feeling frightened and vulnerable.

For example, a child who grows up with a parent battling alcoholism may never experience overt abuse. However, they still live with constant fear, unpredictability, and the sense that they must always be on guard. This chronic stress can rewire the developing brain, leading to heightened anxiety and difficulty regulating emotions later in life.

Then there's neglect. And again, we might picture extreme cases—the child left unfed, unclothed. But emotional neglect can be just as damaging. It's the child whose cries go unanswered, whose feelings are dismissed. It's the child who learns that their needs are a burden, that they're "too much" or "not enough."

Imagine a sensitive child who comes home from school each day bubbling with stories to share, only to be met with a distracted "not now" from their overworked single parent. Over time, that child may learn to suppress their needs and see their desire for connection as an annoyance.

And finally, there are those everyday unmet needs and misattunements. Even in loving families, there are moments when a child's needs can't be perfectly met. And while occasional misattunement is inevitable and not inherently harmful, when it happens repeatedly, it can leave a mark.

It's the sensitive child constantly told to "toughen up." It's the exuberant child chastised for being "too loud." It's the times when our emotions were shut down, our dreams discouraged, and our boundaries violated.

It's important to note that the way these experiences impact us can be profoundly influenced by our intersecting identities. A child of color who experiences racist bullying at school, a queer child whose identity is dismissed or denigrated by family, a child with a disability who is consistently excluded or not accommodated—these layers of marginalization can compound the harm of already painful experiences.

I know this might feel heavy. You might be feeling a surge of grief, anger, or deep sadness for your younger self. Honor those feelings. They're valid and necessary.

But I also want to remind you: Your wounds are not your fault. You were a child, doing the best you could with the resources and resilience you had. And those adults in your life? They were likely operating from their own unhealed wounds.

This isn't about blame. It's about understanding and contextualizing our experiences so we can begin to heal.

And that's where our worksheet comes in. I invite you to take some time to map your personal history and identify those key events and experiences that shaped you. This isn't about crafting a perfect narrative. It's about honoring your story and validating your younger self's reality.

As you work through this exercise, remember to prioritize your emotional safety. Go at your own pace. Take breaks when you need to. Reach out for support if you feel overwhelmed.

It's crucial to challenge some of the common myths and misconceptions about childhood wounds that can hinder our healing. For example, you may have heard the phrase "What doesn't kill you makes you stronger." While adversity can indeed build resilience, this notion can also minimize real pain and suggest that we should be grateful for our wounds. The truth is, we can acknowledge the strength we've gained while also honoring the hurt we've endured.

Similarly, there's a pervasive idea that time heals all wounds. But as anyone who's lived with the lingering effects of childhood pain can attest, time alone is often not enough. Healing requires active work and a willingness to face and process our experiences.

And then there's the belief that talking about painful experiences is "dwelling on the past" or "playing the victim." This couldn't be further from the truth. Acknowledging our wounds is a sign of strength, not weakness. It's a crucial step in reclaiming our stories and our power.

As you prepare to dive into your personal history, remember to lead with self-compassion. Offer your younger self the understanding and validation they craved. Imagine yourself as the loving, attuned parent they needed.

And know that you don't have to do this alone. Working with a therapist or counselor can be incredibly valuable, especially when processing traumatic experiences. They can provide a safe space, guidance, and tools to support your healing journey. If you don't have access to therapy, consider reaching out to trusted friends or family members. Sometimes, simply being heard and validated can be deeply therapeutic.

You're doing profound work, my friend. Acknowledging our origins of pain is a crucial step in the healing journey. It's not easy, but it's so worth it.

Mapping Personal History

Step 1: Create a Safe Space: Before you begin this exercise, ensure you're in a safe, private space where you feel comfortable exploring potentially tender memories. You might want to light a candle, brew a comforting cup of tea, or wrap yourself in a cozy blanket—whatever helps you feel grounded and supported. Consider letting trusted loved ones know that you'll be doing some deep emotional work and might need extra support.

Step 2: Gather Your Materials: You'll need a pen and paper, or you can use a digital document if you prefer. Some people find it helpful to have colored pens or markers on hand, as assigning different colors to different types of experiences can be a useful way to visualize patterns. You might also want to have some tissues nearby, as this process can bring up strong emotions.

Step 3: Set an Intention: Take a few deep breaths and set an intention for this exercise. It might be something like, "I intend to approach my history with curiosity and compassion," or "I intend to validate my younger self's experiences." Choose an intention that resonates with you, and write it down where you can see it throughout the exercise.

Step 4: Map Your Timeline: On your paper, draw a long horizontal line. This represents your life timeline. On the left end, mark your birth. On the right end, mark the present day.

Now, begin to fill in key events and experiences along this timeline. These might include:

- significant family events (births, deaths, marriages, divorces)

- moves or changes in living situation

- traumatic experiences (abuse, neglect, bullying, accidents)

- times when you felt especially loved or supported

- times when you felt neglected, dismissed, or misunderstood

- key moments in your educational journey

- important friendships or relationships

- any other experiences that feel significant to you

Remember, this isn't about creating an exhaustive, chronological record. It's about identifying the experiences that shaped you and left an imprint on your young soul. Don't worry if there are gaps or if the timeline isn't perfectly linear. This is your story, and it doesn't have to be tidy to be valid.

Step 5: Reflect and Journal: Once you've filled in your timeline, take a step back and look at the big picture. What patterns do you notice? Are there certain types of experiences that seem to dominate? How did these experiences make you feel at the time? How do they make you feel now, looking back?

Take some time to journal about what comes up for you. You might want to write a letter to your younger self at different points on the timeline, offering them the words of comfort or validation they needed to hear. For example:

"Dear 8-year-old me, I see how hard you tried to make Mom happy and how you took on responsibilities far beyond your years. I want you to know that it wasn't your job to fix the family. You deserved to be cared for, to have your needs met. You were a wonderful child, and you did the best you could. I'm so proud of you."

Step 6: Offer Compassion: As you reflect on your timeline, you may find yourself feeling a range of emotions—sadness, anger, grief, and even shame. Remind yourself that these feelings are valid and understandable. If shame arises, try to meet it with gentleness. Shame thrives in secrecy; by bringing these experiences to light, you're already loosening its grip.

Offer yourself the compassion you would extend to a dear friend. Place a hand on your heart, and speak kindly to yourself. Recognize the strength and resilience it took for you to survive these experiences. You might say something like:

"I know this is painful to revisit. I'm here with you. Your pain is valid. Your experiences matter. You're not alone."

Step 7: Close With Care: When you feel ready, take a few deep breaths and gently bring your awareness back to the present moment. Thank your younger self for their bravery in sharing their story with you.

Take a moment to do something nurturing for yourself—stretch, take a walk in nature, curl up with a good book. Remind yourself that you are worthy of love and care, just as you are.

Remember, mapping our origins of pain is a process. You might find yourself returning to this exercise multiple times, adding new insights and layers of understanding. Trust the journey. Trust your innate wisdom.

And know that you're not alone. In the next chapter, we'll explore how to acknowledge and validate these experiences, a crucial step in the healing process.

SPECIAL BONUS!

Want this Bonus book for Free?

Get FREE, unlimited access to it and all my new books by joining the Fan Base!

Acknowledgment

In the last chapter, we took a deep dive into our personal histories, mapping out the experiences that shaped our inner child. I know that wasn't easy work. It takes immense courage to face our pain and to look at those wounded parts of ourselves with honesty and openness. I hope you took a moment to acknowledge your bravery and offer yourself some extra tenderness and care.

That kind of self-exploration is not only about understanding where our wounds come from. It's about validating our experiences and saying to our inner child, "I see you. I hear you. What you went through matters."

This is the power of acknowledgment. When we recognize and validate our inner child's experiences, we start to heal the very foundation of our wounds. We begin to rewire those deep-seated beliefs that we're unworthy, unlovable, or fundamentally flawed.

Think about it this way: Imagine if, as a child, every time you felt hurt, scared, or sad, a loving adult sat with you, held you, and said, "I know this is hard. It's okay to feel this way. You're safe and loved, and we'll get through this together." How might that have changed the way you saw yourself and the world?

That's the gift we have the opportunity to give ourselves now. By acknowledging our inner child's pain, we become that loving, attuned parent we always needed. We start to build a new relationship with ourselves, one based on compassion, trust, and unconditional acceptance.

I know this can feel daunting, especially if self-love and self-acceptance don't come naturally to you. So many of us have spent years, even decades, dismissing our own feelings and minimizing our own experiences. We've learned to silence our inner child, push through pain, and put on a brave face.

But I want to invite you to try something different. I want you to start a new dialogue with your inner child, one where their feelings are heard, their experiences are validated, and their needs are met.

This isn't about wallowing in pain or getting stuck in the past. It's about honoring your story, all of it—the joys and the sorrows, the triumphs and the struggles. It's about integrating all the parts of yourself so you can move forward with wholeness and authenticity.

How do we do this? How do we start to acknowledge and validate our inner child's experiences?

One powerful way is through guided reflection. By asking ourselves certain questions and allowing ourselves to sit with the answers, we can start to unravel the stories we've been telling ourselves and begin to weave a new narrative.

I've included some reflection prompts in this chapter to guide you through this process. As you engage with these prompts, remember to approach yourself with curiosity and compassion. There's no right or wrong way to feel or respond. Every part of your experience is valid and worthy of acknowledgment.

You might find some of these prompts bring up strong emotions. That's okay. Those emotions are messengers, telling us which parts of our story need our attention and care. If you need to, take breaks. Breathe deeply. Reach out for support. Trust that you have the strength and resilience to hold your own feelings, even the difficult ones.

As you reflect, you may also notice thoughts of self-judgment or shame arising. This is so common when we start to acknowledge our pain. If this happens, try to meet those thoughts with gentleness. Remind yourself that you were doing the best you could with the resources and understanding you had at the time. Offer your inner child the compassion and understanding they needed then and still need now.

Throughout this process, remember that acknowledgment is an ongoing practice. It's not a one-time event but a continual choice to meet ourselves with honesty and love. Some days, this might feel easy and natural. Other days, it might feel like the hardest thing in the world. Both experiences are okay and normal.

The more we practice acknowledgment, the more we strengthen our capacity for self-love and self-acceptance. We start to trust ourselves more deeply. We begin to show up more authentically in our relationships and in the world. We start to heal, not just our inner child but all the parts of ourselves that have been waiting for our love and attention.

So, dear friend, I invite you to take a deep breath, place a hand on your heart, and turn toward your inner child with openness and love. Let them know that you're here, that you're listening, and that you're ready to honor their story.

Remember, this is sacred work you're doing. It's the work of reclamation, of coming home to yourself. It's not always easy, but it is always, always worth it.

Activity: Guided Reflection Prompts

Find a quiet, comfortable space where you can be alone with your thoughts. You might want to light a candle, put on some soothing music, or brew a comforting cup of tea. Have a journal and pen ready, or use a digital document if you prefer.

Take a few deep breaths, allowing yourself to settle into the present moment. Place a hand on your heart, and send a silent message of love and support to your inner child. Let them know that you're here to listen, understand, and honor their experiences.

Now, gently turn your attention to the following prompts. Read each one slowly, giving yourself plenty of time to reflect and write. Remember, there's no right or wrong way to respond. Let your thoughts and feelings flow freely onto the page.

Reflection Prompts

1. Earliest memory of feeling seen, heard, and validated:

    o   What is your earliest memory of feeling deeply seen, heard, and validated?

        ▪   What did that feel like in your body?

        ▪   What did it teach you about yourself and the world?

2. Feeling dismissed, minimized, or ignored:

    o   Think about a time when your feelings were dismissed, minimized, or ignored:

        ▪   How did that affect you at the time?

        ▪   How does it still impact you today?

3. Messages about worth, lovability, and place in the world:

    o   What messages did you receive as a child, either directly or indirectly, about your:

        ▪   worth

        ▪   lovability

        ▪   place in the world

    o   How have those messages influenced the way you see yourself?

4. Challenging or painful childhood experiences:

    o   Reflect on a challenging or painful experience from your childhood:

        ▪   What did you need most in that moment?

- What would you say to your younger self now, with the wisdom and understanding you have as an adult?

5. Gratitude and pride in childhood experiences:

   o What parts of your childhood experience do you feel most grateful for?

   o What parts are you most proud of yourself for surviving?

6. Visualizing your inner child:

   o Imagine your inner child is standing in front of you:

     - What do they look like?

     - What do they need from you right now?

     - What would you like to say to them?

7. Letting go and cultivating new beliefs

   o What beliefs about yourself and the world are you ready to let go of?

   o What new beliefs would you like to cultivate?

8. Showing up for your inner child daily:

   o How can you start to show up for your inner child on a daily basis?

   o What small acts of love, compassion, and validation can you offer yourself?

9. Letter of acknowledgment to your inner child:

   o Write a letter of acknowledgment to your inner child.

o Let them know that you:

  ▪ see them

  ▪ hear them

  ▪ honor their experiences

o Make a commitment to continue showing up for them with love and compassion.

Checking In

1. As you finish this reflection, take a moment to check in with yourself:

   o How are you feeling?

   o What came up for you?

   o What do you need right now?

2. Honor whatever arises with your gentle, loving attention.

3. Remind yourself that this is a process and that you're doing the best you can.

4. Every moment of acknowledgment, no matter how small, is a step toward healing.

Closing the Practice

1. When you feel ready, slowly bring your awareness back to the present moment.

2. Take a few deep breaths, wiggle your fingers and toes, and gently stretch your body.

3. Consider closing this practice with a physical gesture of self-love and support by:

   a. placing a hand on your heart

   b. giving yourself a hug

   c. speaking a kind affirmation to yourself

4. Let your inner child know that you're in this together, that you'll keep showing up for them, one moment, one day at a time.

Remember:

- You are worthy of your own love and acknowledgment.

- Your experiences matter.

- Your feelings are valid.

- Keep honoring your story, and keep holding space for your healing.

As we conclude this chapter on acknowledging your inner child, I wanted to take a moment to express my deep gratitude for your presence on this journey. Your willingness to show up, dive deep, and meet yourself with such courage and compassion is a gift to witness.

As you continue on this path of healing, I would be honored to hear about your experiences. If you feel called, please consider leaving an honest review of this book, sharing your thoughts, insights, and revelations. Your voice matters, and your story has the power to inspire and uplift others who are just beginning their own inner child healing.

Please know that I receive your feedback with the utmost respect and appreciation. Your truth, in all its raw beauty, is a sacred offering. Thank you for entrusting me with it.

Scan QR code to LEAVE A REVIEW

Part 2:

Techniques for Healing

Welcome to the next stage of your inner child healing journey. Now that we've learned to recognize and acknowledge the wounds of our past, it's time to dive into the transformative work of actively nurturing and caring for our inner child.

In this section, we'll explore powerful techniques for communicating with your inner child, reparenting yourself with love and compassion, and processing and releasing old emotional traumas. You'll learn how to use journaling and inner dialogue to establish a deep, supportive connection with your younger self, mastering the art of soothing old wounds with your own loving presence.

We'll also delve into the concept of reparenting—giving yourself the care, validation, and unconditional love you may have missed as a child. Through this process, you'll discover how to transform your relationship with yourself, becoming the wise, nurturing parent your inner child has always needed.

Finally, we'll introduce you to effective tools for working through and releasing the emotional baggage of the past. With these techniques, you'll be able to safely and gently process old hurts, fears, and traumas, making space for greater peace, joy, and emotional freedom in your life.

Throughout this section, remember that healing is a journey, not a destination. Be patient and compassionate with yourself, celebrating each step forward, no matter how small. Trust that by consistently showing up for your inner child with love and dedication, you are planting the seeds for a profound transformation in your life.

So, take a deep breath, connect with your courage and commitment to your own well-being, and let's dive in. Your inner child is ready to be held, heard, and healed by your own loving embrace.

Communication With the Inner Child

In the last chapter, we explored the profound power of acknowledging our inner child's experiences. We practiced seeing, hearing, and validating the younger parts of ourselves, laying a foundation of self-awareness and self-compassion.

Now, we're going to build on that foundation by learning how to actively communicate with our inner child. This is where the real magic of inner child work begins—in the tender, honest, and deeply healing conversations we can have with our younger selves.

At its core, communicating with your inner child is about creating a safe, loving space for your younger self to express their feelings, needs, and experiences. It's about opening a channel of trust and understanding between your adult self and the child within.

One of the most powerful tools for this kind of communication is journaling. When we put pen to paper (or fingers to keyboard), we tap into a different part of our consciousness. We bypass the critical, judging mind and access a more intuitive, emotional space.

Here's how it might look: Imagine sitting down with your journal and inviting your inner child to speak. You might start with a simple prompt, like "Dear inner child, how are you feeling today?" Then, allow yourself to write freely, without censoring or editing, letting your inner child's voice flow onto the page.

You might be surprised by what emerges. Your inner child may express feelings or memories you weren't consciously aware of. They may share fears, joys, or secret dreams. They may ask for comfort, reassurance, or guidance.

Whatever arises, meet it with openness and compassion. Respond to your inner child's words as you would to a beloved young person in your life—with gentleness, understanding, and unconditional love.

This is the essence of inner dialogue—a written conversation between your adult self and your inner child. It's a way to provide the listening, validation, and loving attention your younger self may have longed for.

As you practice this dialogue, you may find your inner child sharing more and more. They may reveal old wounds, painful memories, or unmet needs. This is a sacred trust—a sign that your inner child feels safe enough to be vulnerable with you.

Honor that trust by continuing to show up with an open heart. Offer your inner child the words of comfort, encouragement, and affirmation they need to hear. Let them know, again and again, that they are seen, heard, and deeply loved.

Over time, this practice of written dialogue can foster a profound sense of emotional connection and intimacy with your inner child. It becomes a way to continually attune to your own needs, feelings, and experiences—a self-nurturing skill that can transform your relationship with yourself.

But journaling is just one tool for communicating with your inner child. You can also practice spoken dialogue, either out loud or in your mind. This might feel awkward at first, but with practice, it can become a powerful way to provide in-the-moment comfort and support to your younger self.

For example, when you notice your inner child feeling scared, overwhelmed, or alone, you might pause and say (silently or aloud), "I'm here with you. You're safe now. We'll get through this together." Or, when you achieve something you're proud of, you might imagine your adult self celebrating with your inner child, saying, "We did it! I'm so proud of us!"

These small moments of connection and communication add up over time, gradually reprogramming your inner dialogue from one of criticism and harshness to one of compassion and love.

Remember, your inner child is a part of you that has always been there and will always be there. By learning to communicate with this precious younger self, you're not just healing old wounds—you're developing a lifelong relationship of trust, understanding, and unconditional positive regard.

This is the gift of inner child communication: a deep, unshakeable sense of being heard, seen, and loved by the most important person in your life: you. As you master the art of this tender self-talk, you'll find old wounds beginning to heal, replaced by a growing sense of wholeness, resilience, and emotional freedom.

So, keep practicing, dear friend. Keep showing up to the page, to the mirror, to the quiet spaces of your own heart, ready to listen and love your inner child. Trust that each conversation, each moment of connection, is weaving a new story of self-compassion and self-trust.

Remember, you are the hero your inner child has been waiting for. You have the power to provide the love, safety, and belonging your younger self has always craved. In doing so, you heal not just your past but your present and future, too.

I'm so proud of you for the work you're doing. Keep going. Keep communicating. Keep loving that beautiful, brave, boundlessly worthy younger you.

Exercise: Inner Child Dialogue

This exercise is designed to help you practice communicating with your inner child through writing. Find a quiet, comfortable space where you can write without interruption. Have your journal and a pen or a computer if you prefer to type.

1. Grounding

   o Close your eyes and take a few deep breaths.

   o Imagine yourself in a safe, beautiful place in nature. This might be a peaceful meadow, a serene beach, or a tranquil forest glade.

- Visualize your inner child in this space with you. See them as clearly as you can—their age, their appearance, their energy.

- Approach your inner child with gentleness and love. Let them know that this is a safe space and that you're here to listen and understand.

2. Inviting Dialogue

- In your journal, write a greeting to your inner child. This might be something like, "Hello, my darling younger self. It's me, your adult self. I'm here to listen to you and to understand. How are you feeling today?"

- Allow your inner child to respond. Write down whatever comes without judging or editing. Let their voice flow freely onto the page.

3. Attuning and Responding

- As your inner child shares, pay attention to their feelings, needs, and experiences.

- Respond to them in writing as you would to a loved child—with empathy, validation, and unconditional positive regard. You might say things like:

  - "I hear you. That must have been so hard."

  - "It's okay to feel angry/sad/scared. Those feelings are valid."

  - "You didn't deserve what happened to you. It wasn't your fault."

  - "I'm here with you now. You're not alone anymore."

- Allow the written conversation to unfold organically, with your adult self providing the listening, understanding, and loving support your inner child needs.

4. Closing and Transitioning

   o   When it feels right, start to bring the dialogue to a close.

   o   Thank your inner child for sharing with you. Reaffirm your love and commitment to them.

   o   You might say something like, "Thank you for trusting me with your feelings and experiences. I'm so proud of you. I love you, and I'm committed to showing up for you, today and always."

   o   Imagine giving your inner child a hug or any other gesture of love and comfort that feels right.

   o   Gently bring your awareness back to the present moment, knowing you can return to this inner space of connection anytime you need to.

5. Reflecting

   o   After the dialogue, take a few moments to write down any reflections or insights that arose for you.

   o   What did you learn about your inner child's needs, feelings, or experiences?

   o   What felt most healing or powerful for you in this process?

   o   How can you integrate this practice of loving inner communication into your daily life?

Remember, this is a practice. It may feel uncomfortable or unfamiliar at first, but with time and repetition, it will start to feel more natural. Trust the process. Trust the wisdom of your own compassionate heart.

Exercise: Mirror Work

Mirror work is a powerful tool for directly communicating with your inner child. It involves speaking to your reflection in a mirror with the love, compassion, and affirmation you would offer to a cherished child. This practice can feel uncomfortable at first, but with time, it can become a profoundly healing way to reparent and nurture your younger self.

Step 1: Preparing: Find a time when you can be alone and undisturbed for at least 15 minutes. Stand or sit in front of a mirror, preferably one where you can see your whole face comfortably. Take a few deep breaths, allowing yourself to settle into the present moment.

Step 2: Seeing Your Inner Child: Look into your own eyes in the mirror. Soften your gaze and try to look beyond your adult self. Imagine seeing your inner child looking back at you. Notice their age, their facial expression, and the look in their eyes. Acknowledge your inner child's presence with a gentle smile or nod. Let them know you see them.

Step 3: Offering Loving Words: Begin to speak to your inner child through the mirror. Use a gentle, loving tone, as you would with a precious young child. Offer words of greeting, love, and reassurance. You might say something like: "Hello, my darling. It's so good to see you." "I'm here with you now. You're safe with me." "I love you so much, just as you are."

Allow your words to flow naturally, trusting that your inner child will hear what they most need to hear.

Step 4: Providing Affirmation and Encouragement: As you continue to speak to your inner child, offer them the affirmation and encouragement they may have lacked in their early life. You might say things like: "I'm so proud of you. You're doing your best, and that's always enough." "It's okay to make mistakes. That's how we learn and grow." "Your feelings are valid. You have a right to feel however you feel." "You are strong, capable, and worthy of love, just as you are."

Really feel the truth of these words as you say them. Let your love and belief in your inner child shine through your eyes and your voice.

Step 5: Closing With Commitment: As you bring the mirror work to a close, reaffirm your ongoing commitment to your inner child. You might say something like: "I'm here for you, always. You can trust me." "I'm committed to taking care of you, to listening to you, and to loving you, no matter what."

Place your hand on your heart as you say these words, physically anchoring your commitment.

Take a few deep breaths, allowing your inner child to really feel your presence and your love.

Step 6: Reflecting and Integrating: After the mirror work, take some time to journal about your experience. What did you notice about your inner child as you looked in the mirror? What emotions did you see in their eyes? What words or phrases felt most powerful or healing for your inner child to hear? How did it feel to offer this kind of loving affirmation to yourself? What resistances or emotions came up for you in the process?

Consider making mirror work a regular part of your inner child communication practice. Even a few minutes a day can make a profound difference in your relationship with your younger self.

Over time, this practice can help rewire your brain, replacing old self-criticism and neglect patterns with new self-love and self-nurturing experiences. It's a way to actively reparent yourself, giving your inner child the loving attention and affirmation they've always needed.

Trust that each time you show up to the mirror with love, you're healing deep wounds and paving the way for a more integrated, compassionate relationship with yourself.

You're doing brave, beautiful work. Keep going. Your inner child is lucky to have you.

Most importantly, trust that each moment of loving connection with your inner child is a profound act of healing. You're doing sacred, life-changing work. Honor yourself for your courage and commitment.

Reparenting the Self

In the last chapter, we explored how to communicate with your inner child, creating a loving dialogue to nurture and heal your younger self. Now, we're going to dive into one of the most transformative aspects of inner child work: reparenting.

Reparenting is the process of giving yourself the love, care, and support you may have missed as a child. It's about becoming the wise, nurturing parent your inner child always needed—providing the safety, validation, and unconditional love that allows your younger self to heal and thrive.

At its core, reparenting is a profound act of self-care. It's a way of meeting your own needs and filling the gaps left by childhood experiences of neglect, misattunement, or absence. By learning to parent ourselves with compassion and consistency, we can rewire old patterns of insecure attachment, building a deep, unshakeable sense of inner security and self-worth.

So, what does reparenting look like in practice? It starts with tuning into your inner child's needs. Just as a loving parent attends to their child's physical, emotional, and psychological well-being, reparenting involves attending to these needs within yourself.

This might mean:

- ensuring you're getting enough rest, nourishment, and physical activity

- creating routines and rituals that provide a sense of safety and predictability

- validating and tending to your own emotions, even the difficult ones

- setting healthy boundaries and learning to say no when needed

- engaging in activities that bring you joy, creativity, and self-expression

- surrounding yourself with supportive, nurturing relationships

- speaking to yourself with kindness, patience, and understanding

Reparenting is about treating yourself with the same tender love and care you would offer a cherished child. It's about learning to prioritize your own needs, comfort yourself in distress, and celebrate yourself in success. It's about becoming your own best parent, mentor, and friend.

One of the key tools in reparenting is developing a personal reparenting plan. This is a concrete, individualized guide for how you will nurture and care for your inner child on a daily basis.

To create your reparenting plan, start by reflecting on what your inner child most needs. What were the experiences or messages you missed out on as a child? What would have helped you feel safe, seen, and loved? Your answers to these questions will help guide your reparenting strategies.

For example, if your inner child craves structure and predictability, your reparenting plan might include:

- establishing regular mealtimes and bedtimes for yourself

- planning out your week in advance, with a balance of work, rest, and play

- creating soothing morning and evening rituals like yoga, journaling, or reading

If your inner child needs more emotional validation and support, your plan might involve:

- scheduling regular check-ins with yourself to ask, "How are you feeling?" and "What do you need?"

- practicing self-compassion and positive self-talk, especially in moments of struggle or failure

- allowing yourself to cry, rage, or express your feelings in safe, healthy ways

- seeking out therapy or supportive friendships to process your emotions

The specifics of your reparenting plan will be unique to you and your inner child's needs. The key is to approach this process with curiosity, openness, and self-compassion. Remember, there's no perfect way to reparent—just as there's no perfect way to parent. What matters is the consistent effort, the daily choice to show up for yourself with love and care.

As you embark on this reparenting journey, be patient with yourself. Changing deep-seated patterns of self-neglect or self-criticism takes time. There will be days when reparenting feels natural and nourishing and others when it feels challenging or even impossible. This is all part of the process.

On the difficult days, remind yourself that each small act of self-care is planting a seed. Even if you can't see the results immediately, trust that you are slowly, steadily reprogramming your inner landscape. Each moment of self-nurturance is teaching your inner child that they are safe, worthy, and deeply loved.

Over time, as you consistently reparent yourself, you may find old wounds beginning to heal. Memories that once felt overwhelming may lose their charge. Triggers that used to send you into a tailspin may become more manageable. You may find yourself feeling more centered, more resilient, more at home in your own skin.

This is the gift of reparenting: a gradual but profound transformation of your relationship with yourself. By becoming the loving parent your inner child always needed, you're not just healing your past—you're reclaiming your present and future. You're learning to love, trust, and care for yourself in a way that ripples out into every area of your life.

So, keep going, dear one. Keep showing up for yourself, day after day, with all the love and dedication you can muster. Trust that you have the wisdom, the strength, and the innate capacity to reparent your inner child. And know that with each act of self-care, you are coming home to yourself in the most beautiful way.

You've got this. Your inner child is so lucky to have you.

Exercise 1: Creating Your Reparenting Plan

This exercise will guide you through the process of creating a personalized reparenting plan. Find a quiet space where you can reflect and write without interruption. Have a journal and pen ready or a blank document on your computer.

1. Connect With Your Inner Child

    o Close your eyes and take a few deep, grounding breaths.

    o Imagine your inner child sitting with you. See them as vividly as you can.

    o Silently ask your inner child what they most need from you. What kind of care, support, or nurturing do they crave?

    o Listen closely to what arises. Trust the wisdom of your intuition.

2. Brainstorm Reparenting Strategies

    o Open your eyes and begin to brainstorm specific ways you can meet your inner child's needs.

    o Consider the different areas of self-care:

        ▪ physical (e.g., nutrition, exercise, rest)

        ▪ emotional (e.g., validation, self-compassion, healthy emotional expression)

- mental (e.g., positive self-talk, boundary setting, therapy)

- spiritual (e.g., meditation, connection with nature, creative pursuits)

o Write down any ideas that come to mind, no matter how small or simple they may seem.

3. Organize Your Plan

o Look over your brainstormed list. Start to organize your ideas into a cohesive plan.

o Divide your plan into daily, weekly, and monthly practices.

o For example:

- Daily: Morning affirmations, 10-minute meditation, nourishing meals

- Weekly: Therapy session, art class, coffee with a supportive friend

- Monthly: Day trip to nature, solo date night, goal-setting session

o Aim for a balance of structure and flexibility. Your plan should feel supportive, not restrictive.

4. Make a Commitment

o Once you've drafted your reparenting plan, read it over. Make any adjustments that feel necessary.

o Then, make a heartfelt commitment to your inner child. You might write something like:

- "Dear [Your Name], I commit to showing up for you every day with love and care. I will honor your needs, validate your feelings, and celebrate your joys. I will be the parent you always needed. You are safe, you are loved, and you are so worthy of this care. I'm here for you, now and always."

- o Sign and date your commitment. Keep it somewhere you can see it regularly as a loving reminder.

5. Implement and Adjust

- o Start implementing your reparenting plan, one day at a time.

- o Notice how each practice feels. What nourishes you? What challenges you?

- o Be open to adjusting your plan as needed. Reparenting is a learning process; what works for you may change over time.

- o Celebrate your successes, no matter how small. Each act of self-care is a victory.

Remember, your reparenting plan is a living document. It will grow and change as you do. The key is to approach it with curiosity, flexibility, and self-compassion.

Trust the process, trust your own innate wisdom, and trust that each loving act of reparenting is healing your inner child in profound and beautiful ways.

You're doing amazing work. Keep going.

Exercise 2: Inner Child Date

One powerful way to reparent your inner child is to take them on regular "dates." This is a time dedicated solely to nurturing and delighting your younger self. Here's how to do it:

1. Set Aside Time

   o Choose a time when you can be alone and uninterrupted for at least an hour.

   o Mark it in your calendar as a sacred commitment to your inner child.

2. Connect With Your Inner Child

   o As the date begins, close your eyes and take a few deep breaths.

   o Imagine your inner child. See their face, their clothes, their energy.

   o Ask them, "What would you like to do together today?" Listen to what arises.

3. Engage in a Nourishing Activity

   o Based on your inner child's desires, choose an activity to do together.

   o This might be something playful, creative, or soothing, such as:

     ▪ coloring or painting

     ▪ building a fort out of blankets

     ▪ going for a nature walk

     ▪ dancing to favorite childhood songs

     ▪ reading beloved children's books

     ▪ cuddling a stuffed animal

o As you engage in the activity, be fully present. Let yourself experience the joy, the curiosity, the absorption of your inner child.

4. Provide Loving Attention

   o Throughout the date, shower your inner child with loving attention.

   o Look at them with adoring eyes. Speak to them with a gentle, encouraging voice.

   o Offer physical affection—hugs, hand-holding, gentle touch.

   o Tell them how much you love them, how proud you are of them, how special they are.

5. Reflect and Journal

   o After the date, take a few moments to reflect on the experience.

   o How did it feel to nurture your inner child in this way? What did you learn about your inner child's needs and desires?

   o Write down any insights or reflections in your journal.

Make inner child dates a regular part of your reparenting practice. Aim to have them at least once a week or more often if your inner child needs extra nourishment.

Remember, the goal is not perfection but loving presence. Your inner child doesn't need a flawless parent; they just need you, showing up with openness, attentiveness, and love.

Each date, no matter how simple, is a profound gift to your inner child. It's a message that they matter, that their needs are important, that they are worthy of love and care.

So, keep dating your inner child. Keep delighting in their company. Keep marveling at the healing power of your own tender attention.

You're giving your inner child the greatest gift of all—the gift of being truly, deeply seen and cherished.

Exercise 3: Reparenting Through Visualization

Visualization is a powerful tool for healing and transformation. By vividly imagining a scene, we can create an almost real experience in our minds that can profoundly affect our emotions, beliefs, and even physiology. In this exercise, we'll use visualization to give your inner child a corrective emotional experience of being parented with love, safety, and attunement.

Step 1: Prepare for the Visualization: Find a quiet, comfortable place where you won't be disturbed. You may want to lie down or sit in a comfortable chair. Have a journal and pen nearby to write down your reflections afterward.

Step 2: Begin to Relax: Close your eyes and take a few deep, slow breaths. With each exhalation, feel your body sinking deeper into relaxation. Imagine a wave of calm washing over you, from the top of your head to the tips of your toes.

Step 3: Meet Your Inner Child: Imagine yourself in a beautiful, peaceful place in nature. This could be a beach, meadow, or forest— wherever you feel safe and serene. In this place, you encounter your inner child. See them as vividly as you can—their age, their appearance, their emotional state. Approach your inner child with a soft, compassionate gaze. Let them know that you are here to take care of them and keep them safe.

Step 4: Offer Loving Interaction: Kneel down to be at eye level with your inner child. Gently ask them, "What do you need right now?" Listen closely to their response. It may come as words, images, or feelings. Based on what your inner child needs, offer a loving interaction. This could be a warm, long hug; soothing words of comfort and reassurance; playful interaction, like dancing, singing, or playing make-believe; or quiet companionship, simply sitting together in peaceful silence.

Allow yourself to fully embody the role of a loving, attuned parent. Offer your inner child your full, devoted attention.

Step 5: Meet a Need: As the interaction unfolds, focus on meeting a specific need of your inner child. If they need to feel safe, imagine wrapping them in a warm, soft blanket of light. If they need to feel seen, reflect back to them their unique qualities and strengths. If they need to feel validated, acknowledge and empathize with their emotions.

Really feel yourself pouring love, care, and nurturance into your inner child. Visualize them soaking it in, their body and energy shifting.

Step 6: Integrate and Close: When it feels right, let the visualization start to come to a close. Thank your inner child for trusting you with their needs. Promise them that you will return and that you are always here for them. Imagine your surroundings starting to fade, bringing your awareness gently back to the present moment.

Take a few deep breaths, wiggle your fingers and toes, and open your eyes when you're ready.

Step 7: Reflect and Journal: Take some time to write about your experience. What did your inner child need most? How did it feel to offer that to them? What emotions arose for you during the visualization? What insights or realizations emerged? How can you integrate this experience into your daily reparenting practice?

Make this visualization a regular part of your inner child work. You might visit your inner child in this way every night before bed or whenever they feel especially in need of nurturing.

Over time, consistent visualizations can have a profound effect. They help rewire your brain, creating new neural pathways associated with safety, love, and secure attachment. They offer your inner child a felt experience of being seen, held, and cherished—an experience they may have missed but one that remains eternally available within your own heart.

Remember, you have everything you need within you to be the loving parent your inner child needs. Trust your instincts and your innate capacity for nurturance and care.

And trust the process. Each visualization, each moment of loving attention, is healing your inner child in ways you may not even realize. You're doing profound, transformative work, one gentle interaction at a time.

Keep going. Your inner child is blossoming under your loving care.

Emotional Processing

In the last chapter, we explored the transformative practice of reparenting—learning to nurture and care for ourselves with the love and attention we may have missed as children. Now, we're going to dive into another crucial aspect of inner child healing: emotional processing.

Emotional processing is the practice of fully acknowledging, feeling, and releasing the painful emotions associated with past traumas and wounds. It's the courageous act of turning towards our pain rather than away from it to heal and integrate these experiences.

For many of us, this can be a daunting prospect. We may have learned early on that certain emotions were not acceptable or safe to express. We may have developed coping mechanisms like emotional numbing, avoidance, or dissociation to protect ourselves from overwhelming feelings.

While these strategies may have helped us survive difficult circumstances, they can also keep us disconnected from our authentic selves and stuck in patterns of emotional pain. Unprocessed emotions don't just disappear; they get stored in our bodies, minds, and spirits, waiting for an opportunity to be acknowledged and released.

This is where the power of emotional processing comes in. By creating a safe, controlled space to feel and express our old pain, we can start to release its hold on us. We can begin to untangle the knots of hurt, fear, and shame that have kept us bound, freeing up energy for healing, growth, and joy.

The science of emotional processing is fascinating. Research has shown that suppressing or avoiding our emotions can lead to a host of negative outcomes, including increased stress, anxiety, and physical health problems. On the other hand, allowing ourselves to feel and express our emotions in a safe and healthy way can lead to improved mental and physical health, better relationships, and increased resilience.

One study, for example, found that individuals who wrote about their deepest thoughts and feelings surrounding traumatic experiences for just 20 minutes a day for four days experienced improvements in both their physical and psychological health. They had fewer doctor's visits, improved immune function, and reduced symptoms of depression and anxiety.

This is because when we process our emotions, we're not just releasing psychological tension but also physical tension. Emotions are, at their core, energy in motion. When we block or suppress this energy, it gets stuck in our bodies, leading to physical symptoms and disease.

By allowing our emotions to flow through us, we're literally freeing up stuck energy, allowing our bodies and minds to return to a state of balance and vitality. We're also integrating the lessons and wisdom of our experiences rather than being controlled by the unresolved pain of the past.

What does emotional processing look like in practice? It can take many forms, depending on your unique needs and preferences. Some common tools include:

1. Journaling

   o Writing about your emotional experiences can be a powerful way to process them.

   o Try free-writing about a painful memory, allowing all your thoughts and feelings to flow onto the page without judgment.

   o You can also write letters to people involved in your past hurts (without necessarily sending them), expressing all the things you never got to say.

   o Another powerful journaling technique is dialoguing with your emotions. Write a conversation between you and your anger, sadness, or fear, asking them what they need and what they're trying to teach you.

2. Art Therapy

    o   Creating art can be a profound way to express emotions that are difficult to put into words.

    o   Try painting, drawing, sculpting, or collaging your feelings.

    o   Focus on the process rather than the product - the goal is to let your emotions move through you, not to create a masterpiece.

    o   You can also try art journaling, combining visual art with written reflections to process your emotions.

3. Movement and Body-Based Practices

    o   Our emotions are deeply connected to our physical bodies.

    o   Practices like yoga, dance, or tai chi can help us release stored emotional energy through movement.

    o   Even simple actions like shaking, stomping, or pushing against a wall can help discharge pent-up feelings.

    o   Try putting on some music and letting your body move however it wants to, without judgment or choreography. Notice what emotions arise and allow them to be expressed through your movement.

4. Crying, Screaming, and Raging

    o   Sometimes, our emotions just need a raw, physical release.

    o   Find a safe, private space where you can let yourself cry, scream into a pillow, or even hit a punching bag.

    o   Allow the sounds and movements to flow through you without stifling them.

o You might feel self-conscious or embarrassed at first, but remember that this is a natural and healthy way to release pent-up emotions. Your body knows what it needs to do to heal.

5. Ritual and Ceremony

   o Creating rituals can be a powerful way to symbolically release past pain.

   o You might write down your painful memories and then burn the paper, letting the ashes represent your emotional release.

   o You might create a ceremony of forgiveness, using objects or actions to symbolize letting go of old resentments.

   o You can also create altars or sacred spaces dedicated to your healing, filling them with objects that represent your journey and your intentions.

Another powerful tool for emotional processing is writing letters.

Exercise: Emotional Release Through Letter Writing

Writing can be a powerful tool for emotional processing, allowing us to express and release feelings that may be difficult to verbalize. This exercise uses letter writing as a way to safely acknowledge and release pent-up emotions.

Step 1: Setting the Stage

Find a quiet, private space where you can write comfortably and without interruption. Gather your materials: paper, a pen (writing by hand can be more cathartic than typing), and any other items that support your emotional processing (tissues, a glass of water, a comforting object, etc.). Before beginning, take a few deep breaths.

Acknowledge that you are creating a safe, confidential space for your emotions to be expressed.

Step 2: Writing the Letter

Think of an emotional wound or traumatic experience that you feel ready to process. This might be a specific event or a general period of your life. Begin to write a letter about this experience, addressed to one of the following:

- yourself at the time of the experience

- another person involved in the experience (a parent, an ex-partner, a childhood bully, etc.)

- the emotion itself (Dear Anger, Dear Shame, etc.)

As you write, let your emotions flow freely onto the page. Don't worry about grammar, spelling, or making sense. The goal is pure, uncensored expression. Write about your memories of the experience, your thoughts and beliefs about what happened, and most importantly, your feelings. Dive deep into the emotional realm: What did you feel at the time? What do you feel now as you remember it? Allow yourself to fully feel and express any anger, sadness, fear, or shame that arises. Validate these feelings as you write. Remind yourself that they are understandable and justified responses to your experience. If you're writing to another person, feel free to express anything you never got to say to them. This is your opportunity to get it all out without fear of judgment or consequences. Keep writing for as long as you need. You might fill pages and pages, or you might feel complete after a few paragraphs. Trust your own process.

Step 3: Releasing and Closing

When you feel a sense of completion, take a moment to reread what you've written. Acknowledge the courage it took to express these deep emotions. Honor the younger version of yourself who experienced this pain and the current version of yourself working to heal it. If you feel called to, you might add a final paragraph offering compassion, validation, or forgiveness to yourself or the other person. Remember, forgiveness doesn't mean condoning hurtful actions; it means releasing the heavy burden of resentment. When you feel ready, find a way to symbolically release the pain you've expressed. You might safely burn the letter, tear it up, or bury it in the ground. As you do, visualize the emotional charge of these experiences being released and neutralized. After releasing the letter, take a few deep breaths. Notice how your body feels. Notice any sense of lightness or relief. To close the exercise, do something nurturing for yourself. Take a warm bath, make a cup of soothing tea, or call a supportive friend. Acknowledge that you've done brave and important work.

Step 4: Integrating and Reflecting

In the days following this exercise, pay attention to any shifts in your emotions or perspective. You may find that you feel a sense of closure or resolution around the experience you wrote about. Be gentle with yourself as you integrate this emotional release. You may feel raw or vulnerable for a while. This is normal and a sign that deep healing is happening. If intense emotions continue to surface, consider repeating this exercise or reaching out for additional support from a therapist or counselor. In your journal, reflect on your experience with this exercise: What did you learn about yourself and your emotions? What felt challenging? What felt liberating? Remember that emotional processing is an ongoing journey. Celebrate each step you take towards healing, and trust that each courageous expression brings you closer to wholeness.

One particularly powerful tool for emotional processing is guided imagery. Guided imagery involves using your imagination to create healing internal experiences. By vividly picturing and engaging with symbolic scenes and actions, you can help your mind and body process emotions in a safe, controlled way.

The power of guided imagery lies in the fact that our brains don't distinguish much between real and imagined experiences. When we vividly imagine a scene, our brains respond as if it's actually happening, firing the same neurons and creating the same emotional and physiological responses.

This means that we can use guided imagery to give ourselves corrective emotional experiences. We can imagine ourselves feeling safe, loved, and empowered, and our brains will respond by creating those feelings in reality. Over time, this can help rewire our neural pathways, replacing old patterns of fear and pain with new experiences of healing and wholeness.

Here is a step-by-step guided imagery exercise for processing and releasing emotional pain:

Guided Imagery Exercise: The Healing Pool

1. Preparing

    o   Find a quiet, comfortable place where you won't be disturbed.

    o   Sit or lie down in a position that allows you to relax.

    o   You may want to have some tissues, a glass of water, and a journal nearby.

    o   If it feels comfortable for you, place one hand on your heart and one on your belly, connecting with your own loving, nurturing touch.

2. Relaxing

    o   Close your eyes and take a few deep, slow breaths.

    o   With each exhalation, imagine yourself releasing tension and settling more deeply into relaxation.

    o   Starting at the top of your head and moving down to your toes, mentally scan your body, noticing any areas of tightness or discomfort.

    o   As you notice these areas, imagine breathing into them, allowing them to soften and relax.

- You might visualize a warm, golden light moving through your body, dissolving any remaining tension and filling you with a sense of peace and safety.

3. Visualizing the Healing Pool

- Imagine yourself walking on a peaceful path through a beautiful forest.

- Take in all the details of your surroundings—the colors of the leaves, the texture of the earth beneath your feet, the sounds of birds and gentle breezes.

- As you walk, you come to a clearing. In the center of the clearing is a large, crystal-clear pool of water.

- The pool is surrounded by lush, green grass and beautiful, fragrant flowers. You can hear the gentle sound of a waterfall cascading into the far end of the pool.

- You approach the edge of the pool. As you look into the water, you can see that it's the perfect temperature and depth for you.

- You have a deep, intuitive sense that this is a magical, healing pool. Its waters have the power to cleanse and release any emotional pain you're ready to let go of.

4. Entering the Pool

- When you feel ready, start to wade into the pool.

- As you do, imagine naming the emotions or experiences you want to release. You might say, "I am releasing the sadness from [experience]" or "I am letting go of the anger I felt toward [person]."

- With each step into the water, feel these emotions start to flow out of you. Imagine them as a dark, heavy substance leaving your body and dissolving in the clear water.

- o Keep wading in until you are fully immersed, with the water supporting and surrounding you.

- o Take a moment to feel the sensation of being held and supported by the water. Allow yourself to relax into its gentle embrace.

5. Cleansing

- o As you float in the healing pool, imagine the water infusing every cell of your body.

- o Feel it gently dissolving any remaining emotional residue, cleansing your mind, body, and spirit.

- o If specific memories or images arise, allow them to appear on the surface of the water and then gently float away, releasing their charge.

- o You might imagine the waterfall at the end of the pool washing over you, rinsing away any lingering traces of pain or negativity.

- o Stay in the pool for as long as you need, letting the water continue its healing work. Trust that you are safe to feel and release whatever needs to come up.

6. Emerging Renewed

- o When you feel a sense of completion, start to make your way back to the edge of the pool.

- o As you emerge from the water, take a moment to notice how your body feels. Are there areas that feel lighter, more spacious, or more energized?

o Look down at your skin and imagine seeing it glowing with health and vitality, cleansed of any residual emotional toxins.

o Take a deep breath and feel the freshness and vitality of the air filling your lungs. It's as if you're breathing in pure renewal and healing.

o As you step out of the pool and back onto the grass, feel the earth beneath your feet, grounding and supporting you.

o Take a moment to appreciate this sense of renewal and freedom. You have courageously released what was no longer serving you. You have made space for new growth and joy.

7. Returning and Reflecting

o When you're ready, start to bring your attention back to the room you're in.

o Take a few deep breaths, wiggle your fingers and toes, and gently open your eyes.

o Take some time to journal about your experience. What emotions came up for you? What did you release? How do you feel now?

o Be sure to drink some water and take care of yourself after this deep work. You might want to rest, nourish yourself with healthy food, or engage in a calming activity like gentle stretching or listening to soothing music.

Remember, emotional processing is a brave and powerful act. It takes immense courage to face our old pain and allow ourselves to feel it fully. Honor your own timing and capacity. Some days, you may feel ready to dive deep, while other days, you may need to take a gentler approach.

Trust the wisdom of your own psyche. Your mind and body know how to heal. By creating safe, loving spaces for your emotions to be felt and released, you're allowing this innate healing process to unfold.

If intense emotions arise during or after this process, remember that this is normal and okay. Emotions are energy, and sometimes, they need to move through us vigorously before they can be released. If you feel overwhelmed, remember that you can always pause, take a break, or reach out for support.

It's also important to balance emotional processing with practices that ground and stabilize you. After a deep session, do something that helps you feel safe and connected to the present moment. This might be drinking a warm cup of tea, cuddling with a pet, or calling a supportive friend.

As you continue on your emotional processing journey, be sure to celebrate your progress. Each time you courageously face and release a piece of old pain, you're one step closer to wholeness. You're reclaiming your birthright to live with a free, open, and joyful heart.

And remember, you're not alone in this deep work. So many others are walking this path of healing alongside you. Consider reaching out for support from a therapist, a trusted friend, or a supportive community. Sharing our stories and bearing witness to each other's pain can be profoundly healing.

Keep going, courageous one. Keep honoring your emotions and trusting your process. With each step, you're reclaiming your wholeness, vitality, and birthright to live with a free and open heart.

Your inner child thanks you. Your future self thanks you. And I thank you for your immense bravery and dedication to your healing.

Part 3:

Transforming the Self

Welcome to the transformative part of your inner child healing journey. In the previous sections, we delved into recognizing and healing the wounds of the past. Now, it's time to actively reshape your present and future by rewriting your inner narrative, building empowering new beliefs, and cultivating emotional resilience.

In this section, you'll learn powerful techniques to shift your inner dialogue from critical and limiting to supportive and expansive. Through engaging activities and exercises, you'll craft new affirmations and narratives that align with your highest potential and deepest truth.

We'll also guide you through the process of identifying and replacing old, limiting beliefs with empowering new ones. You'll engage in transformative belief restructuring exercises that will help you rewire your mind for success, joy, and inner peace.

Finally, we'll share proven strategies for developing emotional resilience—the ability to bounce back from challenges and thrive in the face of adversity. Through resilience-building activities and daily challenges, you'll strengthen your emotional muscles and cultivate unshakeable inner strength.

Throughout this section, remember that transformation is a process, not an event. Be patient and compassionate with yourself as you learn and grow. Celebrate each step forward, no matter how small, knowing that you're moving toward a more empowered, joyful, and authentic version of yourself.

Get ready to let go of who you thought you were and embrace the magnificent being you were always meant to be. Your inner child is cheering you on, ready to emerge into the light of your limitless potential.

Let's begin this transformative journey together.

Changing the Narrative

In the last chapter, we explored the profound practice of emotional processing—courageously feeling and releasing the painful emotions of the past. Now, we're going to focus on actively reshaping your inner dialogue, the constant stream of thoughts and stories you tell yourself about who you are and what's possible for you.

For many of us, our inner dialogue has been shaped by the wounds and traumas of our past. If we experienced criticism, neglect, or abuse as children, we may have internalized those voices, adopting a harsh, judgmental tone towards ourselves. We may constantly tell ourselves that we're not good enough, that we're unworthy of love and success, and that we're destined to fail.

These negative narratives can be incredibly powerful, shaping our beliefs, actions, and life experiences. When we constantly tell ourselves we're not capable, we're less likely to take risks or pursue our dreams. When we believe we're unlovable, we may sabotage relationships or settle for less than we deserve.

But here's the good news: Just as our narratives have been learned, they can also be unlearned. We have the power to consciously rewrite our inner dialogue, replacing those critical, limiting stories with ones that are supportive, empowering, and aligned with our deepest truth.

The first step in changing your narrative is awareness. Start to notice the thoughts you have about yourself throughout the day. What's the general tone of your inner dialogue? Is it kind and encouraging, or harsh and critical? Do your thoughts lift you up or weigh you down?

One powerful way to build this awareness is to keep a thought journal. For a few days, commit to writing down your self-talk, especially in challenging or triggering situations. Don't censor or judge what you write; the goal is simply to observe and acknowledge your current patterns.

As you review your thought journal, you may start to notice common themes or recurring phrases. Maybe you constantly tell yourself, "I can't handle this" when stressed, or "I'm so stupid" when you make a mistake. These recurring thoughts are like scripts that your mind automatically plays out, often without conscious awareness.

Once you've identified your negative scripts, you can start to consciously rewrite them. This is where the power of affirmations comes in. Affirmations are positive statements that you repeat to yourself, with the goal of internalizing them as beliefs.

The key to effective affirmations is to craft them as if they're already true, even if they don't feel true yet. So, instead of "I will be confident," you might say, "I am confident and capable." Instead of "I want to be loved," you might affirm, "I am worthy of love just as I am."

It's also essential that your affirmations feel authentic and believable to you. If your current self-talk is "I'm a failure," jumping straight to "I'm a massive success" might feel too far of a stretch. Instead, you might start with "I am learning and growing every day" or "I have unique gifts to offer the world."

As you craft your affirmations, consider all the domains of your life— your relationships, career, health, and spirituality. Create affirmations that support your highest vision in each area.

Here are some examples of transformative affirmations:

- "I deeply and completely love and accept myself."

- "I trust in my ability to handle whatever comes my way."

- "I am open to abundance and opportunity flowing to me."

- "I forgive myself for past mistakes and trust in my ability to learn and grow."

- "I am grateful for my body and treat it with kindness and respect."

- "I am surrounded by love and support."

- "I am safe, I am calm, I am at peace."

Once you've crafted your affirmations, the real work begins: the daily practice of replacing your old narratives with these new, empowering truths. This takes commitment and consistency, but over time, it can profoundly transform your inner landscape and outer life experiences.

One simple but powerful practice is affirmation meditation. Sit quietly, close your eyes, and repeat your affirmations to yourself, either out loud or silently. Really feel the truth of these statements resonating in your body. Visualize yourself embodying these qualities, living from this empowered place.

You can also place your affirmations around your environment: on sticky notes on your mirror, as the background on your phone, or even on your coffee mug. The more you see and repeat these positive statements, the more they'll start to feel like your natural way of thinking.

Another powerful way to shift your inner dialogue is to directly engage with your inner critic.

Exercise: Dialogue With Your Inner Critic

This exercise involves directly engaging with your inner critic—the voice inside your head that judges, criticizes, or undermines you. By having a conscious dialogue with this voice, you can start to understand its origins, challenge its assumptions, and, ultimately, transform its message.

Step 1: Identifying Your Inner Critic

Recall a recent situation where your inner critic was particularly loud or harsh. What was the situation, and what specific thoughts or judgments did your inner critic express? Write down these critical thoughts verbatim without editing or softening them. For example: "You're so lazy. You'll never amount to anything." Notice the tone of these thoughts. Is your inner critic angry, mocking, or disapproving? Does it remind you of anyone from your past?

Step 2: Engaging in Dialogue

Now, imagine you could have a direct conversation with your inner critic. What would you say in response to its judgments? Write out this dialogue, letting it flow naturally. For example: Inner Critic: "You're so lazy. You'll never amount to anything." You: "I hear your frustration, but I don't agree with your assessment. I'm working hard and making progress, even if it's not always visible."

Challenge your inner critic's assumptions and generalizations. Ask for specific evidence to support its claims. For example: You: "What evidence do you have that I'll never amount to anything? I can think of many instances where I've achieved my goals and made a positive impact."

Express compassion for your inner critic. Recognize that it likely developed as a way to protect you or help you survive difficult circumstances. For example: You: "I know you're trying to motivate me and keep me safe from failure or rejection. But your harsh words are actually holding me back. I need a different kind of motivation— one that comes from self-love and belief in my potential."

Step 3: Transforming the Critic Into a Coach

Now, imagine transforming your inner critic into an inner coach—a wise, compassionate voice that supports and encourages you. Rewrite your inner critic's original statements from this new, supportive perspective. For example: Inner Coach: "I see how hard you're working. Every effort counts, and every challenge is an opportunity to grow. You're capable of amazing things, and I'm here to remind you of that."

Engage in a new dialogue with your inner coach. What advice, encouragement, or perspective does it offer? For example: You: "I'm feeling stuck and unsure of my next steps." Inner Coach: "That's a normal part of the journey. Trust your intuition and take one small step at a time. You have the resilience and creativity to navigate this. I believe in you."

Step 4: Integrating and Practicing

Reflect on your experience with this exercise. What insights did you gain about your inner critic? What shifted when you engaged it in direct dialogue? Consider giving your inner coach a name or even visualizing it as a particular character or symbol. This can help you invoke its presence more easily. Practice calling on your inner coach's wisdom and encouragement, especially in moments when your inner critic is loud. Commit to having the final word come from your coach, not your critic. Over time, notice how the tone and content of your inner dialogue start to shift. Celebrate each moment of self-compassion and self-encouragement.

Additionally, storytelling is another powerful tool for changing your narrative. Our lives are essentially stories that we tell ourselves and others. If your current life story is one of limitation, victimhood, or struggle, know that you have the power to rewrite it.

Start crafting a new life story for yourself, one in which you are the hero, courageously overcoming challenges and moving towards your highest vision. This doesn't mean denying or bypassing the hard parts of your journey but reframing them as opportunities for growth, resilience, and wisdom.

For example, instead of telling the story of how your childhood traumas have indefinitely broken you, you might tell the story of how these experiences have given you unique strengths, insights, and a capacity for deep empathy and connection. Instead of the story of how you'll never find love, you might tell the story of how each relationship, even the painful ones, has taught you valuable lessons and brought you closer to the love you deserve.

As you begin to live into these new, empowering stories, you'll find your reality starting to shift to match them. You'll start to attract people and opportunities that align with your highest vision. You'll find yourself taking actions that you previously thought were impossible.

You'll meet challenges with a sense of resilience and faith in your ability to overcome them.

Remember, changing your narrative is a process, not a one-time event. There will be days when your old stories and critical voices seem to shout louder than your new, empowering ones. This is normal and okay. The goal is not perfection but practice—the daily commitment to choosing thoughts and stories that lift you up rather than tear you down.

Be patient and compassionate with yourself on this journey. Celebrate each moment of awareness, each loving thought, each courageous reframing of your story. Trust that each affirmation, each empowering story, is planting a seed of transformation that will blossom in perfect timing.

And remember, you are not alone in this process. Reach out for support from loved ones, a therapist or coach, or communities that uplift and inspire you. Share your journey with others and allow their belief in you to fuel your own.

Keep going, dear one. Keep choosing thoughts and stories that honor your innate worthiness, boundless potential, and fundamental goodness. In time, these new narratives will become your default way of being, effortlessly guiding you toward a life of joy, meaning, and authentic self-expression.

Your inner child is listening to every word you say to yourself. Make those words ones of love, encouragement, and unwavering belief. In doing so, you heal not just yourself but all those who have the gift of witnessing your journey.

I believe in you and the story you're courageously writing. Keep shining.

Activity: Crafting New Affirmations and Narratives

This activity will guide you through the process of identifying your current limiting narratives and replacing them with empowering affirmations and stories. You'll need a journal and a quiet space where you can reflect and write without interruption.

Step 1: Identifying Limiting Narratives

1. Think about the areas of your life where you feel stuck, dissatisfied, or self-critical. This might be your relationships, career, health, self-image, etc.

2. For each area, write down the dominant stories or narratives you tell yourself. For example:

   o "I'm not good enough for a loving relationship."

   o "I'll never be successful in my career."

   o "I'm too old/too fat/too [insert self-judgment] to be happy and healthy."

3. Notice the common themes or beliefs underlying these narratives. Do you see patterns of unworthiness, unlovability, limitation, or fear?

4. Reflect on the origins of these narratives. Can you trace them back to specific experiences or messages from your past?

Step 2: Crafting Empowering Affirmations

1. For each limiting narrative you identified, write down a counter-affirmation—a positive statement that directly challenges or reframes the limiting belief. For example:

   o "I am worthy of love and respect in all my relationships."

   o "I have unique talents and skills that bring value to my career."

   o "I embrace my body and treat it with kindness and care."

2. Make sure your affirmations are phrased in the present tense, as if they're already true. Start each one with "I am," "I have," or "I choose."

3. Ensure that your affirmations feel authentic and believable to you. If they feel too far from your current reality, adjust them to be more gradual or incremental.

4. Read your affirmations out loud. Notice how they feel in your body. Do they evoke a sense of expansion, relief, or empowerment? If not, keep refining them until they resonate deeply.

5. Choose 3-5 affirmations to focus on for the next 30 days. Write them down where you'll see them often—in your journal, on your bathroom mirror, as the lock screen on your phone, etc.

Step 3: Rewriting Your Life Story

1. Reflect on your current life story—the overarching narrative you tell yourself and others about who you are and what your life has been about.

2. Notice where this story might be limiting, disempowering, or one-dimensional. Are you casting yourself as a victim, a failure, a helpless bystander in your own life?

3. Now, imagine you're writing your life story as a hero's journey. You are the protagonist, facing challenges and overcoming obstacles on your path to growth and transformation.

4. Rewrite key chapters or defining moments of your life from this empowered perspective. For example:

    o Instead of "My divorce devastated me and proved I'm unlovable," you might write, "My divorce was a difficult but transformative experience that taught me resilience, self-love, and the importance of honoring my own needs."

o Instead of "I failed at my business, proving I'm not cut out for success," you might write, "Starting my own business was a courageous learning experience that developed my skills, clarified my values, and prepared me for future successes."

5. As you rewrite your story, look for the gifts, lessons, and unexpected blessings in even the hardest parts of your journey. How have your challenges made you stronger, wiser, and more compassionate?

6. Write a new chapter for your future, one that aligns with your highest aspirations and deepest values. What kind of life do you want to create? What impact do you want to have? What qualities do you want to embody?

7. Commit to living into this new story, one day and one choice at a time. When you face challenges or setbacks, ask yourself: "How would the hero of my story respond to this? What would my best self do?"

Step 4: Reflecting and Integrating

1. After completing this activity, take some time to reflect on your experience. What insights arose for you? What feels most challenging about changing your narratives? What feels most exciting or liberating?

2. Consider sharing your new affirmations and life story with a trusted friend, therapist, or coach. Invite them to hold you accountable and remind you of your new narratives, especially when old patterns resurface.

Remember, changing your narrative is an ongoing practice. Be patient and compassionate with yourself as you learn to think and speak about yourself in new ways. Trust that every loving affirmation, every empowered story, is reshaping your brain and your life for the better.

Keep going, storyteller. Your words have the power to create worlds, both within and without. Choose them wisely, and watch as your reality transforms to match the magic of your imagination.

Building New Beliefs

Our beliefs are the fundamental assumptions we hold about ourselves, others, and the world around us. They are the lenses through which we interpret our experiences, the foundations upon which we build our thoughts, feelings, and actions.

Just like our inner narratives, many of our beliefs are formed in childhood, shaped by our early experiences and the messages we received from others. If we grew up in an environment of criticism, scarcity, or fear, we may have developed beliefs like "I'm not good enough," "There's never enough," or "The world is a dangerous place."

While once adaptive and even necessary for our survival, these beliefs can limit us in adulthood, keeping us stuck in patterns of self-doubt and anxiety and holding us back from our full potential. They can be like invisible chains, constraining our joy, our relationships, and our success.

But just like any learning, beliefs can be unlearned. We have the power to consciously examine our beliefs, to question their validity, and to replace those that no longer serve us with new, empowering beliefs that support our growth and happiness.

The first step in this process is awareness. Start to notice the beliefs that underlie your thoughts and reactions, especially in challenging situations. For example, if you find yourself feeling anxious about a job interview, you might have a core belief of "I'm not competent enough." If you shy away from expressing your needs in relationships, you may hold a belief that "My needs are not important."

One powerful way to uncover your core beliefs is to use the "Downward Arrow" technique. This involves starting with a negative thought and then continually asking yourself, "If that thought were true, what would it mean about me?" until you arrive at a core belief.

For example:

1. Negative thought: "I messed up that presentation at work."

2. What would that mean about you? "It means I'm not good at my job."

3. And if that were true, what would that mean about you? "It means I'm a failure."

4. And if that were true, what would that mean about you? "It means I'm not good enough."

In this example, the core belief is "I'm not good enough." This is a common limiting belief that can fuel perfectionism, procrastination, and self-sabotage.

Once you've identified a limiting belief, the next step is to challenge it. Just because you've believed something for a long time doesn't mean it's true. In fact, many of our beliefs are distorted, exaggerated, or simply outdated.

To challenge a belief, look for evidence that contradicts it. For the belief "I'm not good enough," you might list your accomplishments, the times you've received positive feedback, and the unique skills and qualities you possess. You might also look for counterexamples— people who are successful and happy, who aren't perfect, or who have faced similar challenges.

Another way to challenge beliefs is to examine their impact on your life. Ask yourself: "How does believing this hold me back? What could be possible if I let go of this belief? Is this belief aligned with my deepest values and goals?"

As you start to loosen the grip of your old, limiting beliefs, you create space for new, empowering beliefs to take root. This is where the real magic happens—where you get to consciously choose the beliefs that will shape your reality moving forward.

To create new beliefs, start by envisioning the life you want to create— the relationships, the career, the sense of purpose and joy. What would you need to believe about yourself and the world to create this reality?

Some examples of empowering beliefs might be:

- "I am capable of learning and growing."

- "I am worthy of love and respect."

- "I trust in my ability to handle challenges."

- "There is abundance available to me."

- "My uniqueness is my strength."

- "I am resilient and can bounce back from setbacks."

As you craft your new beliefs, ensure they are phrased in the present tense, as if they are already true. Make them specific, personal, and emotionally resonant. Most importantly, make sure they feel expansive and liberating—like they're opening up new possibilities rather than boxing you in.

Once you've identified your new beliefs, the real work begins: the daily practice of embodying and reinforcing them. This is where belief restructuring exercises come in.

One powerful exercise is called "Acting As If." This involves choosing a new belief and then acting, thinking, and feeling as if it were already 100% true. For example, if your new belief is "I am worthy of love and respect," you might start setting boundaries in your relationships, expressing your needs clearly, and treating yourself with compassion and care.

The key to "Acting As If" is consistency and repetition. The more you align your actions with your new belief, the more your brain will begin accept it as reality. Over time, what once felt like pretending will start to feel like your natural way of being.

Another powerful belief restructuring exercise is visualization. This involves vividly imagining yourself living from your new beliefs and experiencing the emotional and sensory details of this reality.

For example, if your new belief is "I am capable of learning and growing," you might visualize yourself taking on a new challenge with confidence and curiosity. See yourself putting in the effort, bouncing back from obstacles, and ultimately succeeding. Feel the pride, the excitement, the sense of expansion in your body.

The more vividly and consistently you visualize, the more you're training your brain to accept your new beliefs as truth. You're literally rewiring your neural pathways, creating a new default mode of thinking and being.

As you work to integrate your new beliefs, be patient and compassionate with yourself. Remember that you're undoing years, possibly decades, of conditioning. There will be times when your old beliefs resurface, when doubt and fear creep back in. This is normal and doesn't mean you're failing.

In these moments, return to your belief restructuring exercises. Remind yourself of the evidence supporting your new beliefs. Act as if, even if you don't fully feel it yet. Lean on affirmations and visualization to reinforce your new mental patterns.

Over time, with consistent practice, your new beliefs will start to feel more and more natural. You'll find yourself responding to challenges with greater resilience and resourcefulness. You'll catch yourself thinking thoughts of self-love and possibility rather than self-doubt and limitation. You'll start attracting people and experiences that match your new vibration.

This is the transformative power of changing your beliefs; it literally changes your reality. By choosing to believe in your own worthiness, competence, and potential, you open up a whole new world of possibility.

So, keep going, belief warrior. Keep examining, challenging, and consciously choosing the beliefs that will propel you forward. Trust that every aligned action, every empowered thought, is reshaping your identity and your life in profound ways.

Your inner child is watching and learning from your example. Show them what it looks like to believe in oneself wholeheartedly, to rise above limiting conditioning and live from a place of authentic power.

In doing so, you heal not just your own life but the lineage of beliefs in your family and community.

Worksheet: Belief Restructuring Exercises

This worksheet will guide you through a series of exercises designed to help you identify, challenge, and replace your limiting beliefs with empowering ones. You'll need a journal and a quiet space where you can reflect and write without interruption.

Exercise 1: Identifying Limiting Beliefs

1. List areas of your life where you feel stuck, challenged, or unfulfilled. This might include relationships, career, health, finances, self-image, etc.

2. For each area, ask yourself: "What do I believe about myself in relation to this area? What do I believe is or isn't possible for me?"

3. Write down the beliefs that emerge. Be honest and uncensored, even if the beliefs seem irrational or harsh.

4. For each belief, ask yourself: "Where did this belief come from? How long have I been carrying it? How has it impacted my life so far?"

5. Reflect on the emotional charge each belief holds. How do you feel when you think about or act based on this belief?

Exercise 2: Challenging Limiting Beliefs

1. Choose one limiting belief to focus on for this exercise.

2. Write down all the evidence you can find that contradicts this belief. This might include accomplishments, compliments you've received, times when you've overcome challenges, etc.

3. Now, write down the evidence you've been using to support the belief. Examine this evidence critically. Is it factual, or is it based on assumptions or past conditioning?

4. Imagine a friend or loved one held this same limiting belief about themselves. What would you say to them? How would you encourage them to see their situation differently?

5. Consider the impact of this belief. How has it limited you or held you back? What could be possible if you let go of it?

Exercise 3: Creating Empowering Beliefs

1. Review the areas of life you identified in Exercise 1. For each area, ask yourself: "What would I like to experience in this area? What would I need to believe about myself and life to create this reality?"

2. Write down the new, empowering beliefs that emerge. Phrase them in the present tense, as if they're already true.

3. For each new belief, engage your senses. What would it look like, feel like, sound like to fully embody this belief? Write down the details.

4. Create an affirmation or mantra for each new belief. This should be a short, powerful statement that encapsulates the essence of the belief.

5. Identify one small action you can take, starting today, to align with each new belief. This could be an internal action (like repeating your affirmation) or an external action (like setting a boundary or trying something new).

Exercise 4: Acting "As If"

1. Choose one of your new, empowering beliefs to focus on for this exercise.

2. For the next week, commit to acting as if this belief were already 100% true. This means making decisions, taking actions, and engaging in self-talk that aligns with the belief.

3. Each day, journal about your experience. What actions did you take? How did it feel? What resistance or fears came up?

4. At the end of the week, reflect on how embodying this belief has impacted your life. What new insights or experiences emerged? How can you continue to integrate this belief moving forward?

Exercise 5: Belief Visualization

1. Choose another one of your new, empowering beliefs to work with.

2. Find a quiet, comfortable space where you can relax without interruption. Close your eyes and take a few deep, grounding breaths.

3. Begin to visualize yourself fully embodying this belief. See yourself thinking, feeling, and acting in alignment with it.

4. Engage all your senses in the visualization. What do you see, hear, feel, taste, and smell in this reality where your new belief is true?

5. Allow yourself to feel the positive emotions associated with this belief—the joy, the confidence, the peace, the excitement.

6. Anchor this feeling in your body with a physical gesture, like touching your heart or squeezing your fist. This anchor will help you recall the feeling of the belief even when you're not actively visualizing.

7. Gently open your eyes and return to the present moment. Take a few minutes to journal about your experience.

8. Repeat this visualization daily for at least a week, using your physical anchor to recall the feeling throughout your day.

Exercise 6: Belief Bridge

The "Belief Bridge" exercise helps you navigate the transition from your old, limiting beliefs to your new, empowering ones. It acknowledges that change is a process and provides a structured way to gradually shift your thinking.

1. Identify the belief gap. Review your list of limiting beliefs from Exercise 1 and your list of empowering beliefs from Exercise 3. For each set of old and new beliefs, assess the gap between them. How big of a leap is it from the old belief to the new one? For example, if your old belief is "I'm unlovable," and your new belief is "I am worthy of abundant love," the gap is quite significant.

2. Create belief bridges. For each set of beliefs, create a series of "bridge beliefs" that gradually close the gap between the old and new beliefs. Bridge beliefs should be statements that are a little bit more believable than your new belief but still a step in the direction of your desired thinking. For the example above, a bridge belief might be "I am learning to love and accept myself" or "I am open to the possibility of being loved." Create as many bridge beliefs as you need to feel like you're making manageable, believable steps.

3. Practice crossing the bridge. Start by affirming your first bridge belief. Repeat it to yourself daily, look for evidence to support it, and act as if it's true (as you did in Exercises 4 and 5). Once the first bridge belief starts to feel more natural and automatic, move on to the next one. Continue this process, gradually working your way towards your ultimate empowering belief.

4. Reflect on the journey. As you work with your belief bridges, be patient and compassionate with yourself. Remember that you're undoing years of conditioning. Celebrate each step you take across the bridge, each shift toward more loving and

empowering thinking. If you find yourself slipping back into old beliefs, simply acknowledge it and gently guide yourself back to your current bridge belief. Trust that every repetition and affirmation is reshaping your neural pathways and bringing you closer to fully embodying your new beliefs.

Integration and Reflection

After completing these exercises, take some time to reflect on your journey. What have you learned about your beliefs and their impact on your life? What new possibilities are opening up as you shift your beliefs?

Remember that changing your beliefs is an ongoing process. Keep returning to these exercises, especially when you feel stuck or challenged. Celebrate each step forward, no matter how small, knowing that you are rewiring your brain and reshaping your reality with every repetition.

Consider sharing your journey with a trusted friend or community. Surrounding yourself with people who support your growth and mirror your new beliefs can be incredibly reinforcing.

Above all, trust the process. Trust that as you align your beliefs with your deepest truth and highest potential, life will begin to align in miraculous ways. You are co-creating your reality with every thought, every belief, every action.

Choose wisely, and watch as your world transforms from the inside out.

Developing Emotional Resilience

In the last chapter, we dove deep into the transformative power of building new beliefs—the foundational assumptions that shape our thoughts, feelings, and actions. Now, we're going to focus on developing emotional resilience—the capacity to adapt and thrive in the face of life's inevitable challenges and stressors.

Emotional resilience is like a muscle. Just as we can strengthen our physical muscles through exercise and training, we can build our emotional resilience through specific strategies and practices. The more we flex our resilience muscle, the more capable we become of bouncing back from setbacks, managing stress, and maintaining a sense of well-being even in difficult times.

Developing emotional resilience is particularly important for those of us on a journey of inner child healing. Many of us have experienced traumas or adversities that have made us feel vulnerable, powerless, or even broken. We may have developed coping mechanisms that helped us survive in the short term but limit our ability to thrive in the long term.

By building our emotional resilience, we reclaim our inner strength. We learn to trust in our ability to handle life's ups and downs. We develop a sense of emotional flexibility and adaptability that allows us to meet challenges with grace and grit.

So, what are some strategies for strengthening emotional resilience? Here are a few key practices:

1. Mindfulness

    o Mindfulness is the practice of bringing our attention to the present moment with openness and non-judgment.

    o By learning to observe our thoughts and feelings without getting swept away by them, we increase our capacity to respond rather than react to stressors.

- o Mindfulness practices like meditation, deep breathing, and body scans can help us cultivate a sense of inner calm and clarity even in the midst of chaos.

2. Self-Awareness

- o Self-awareness involves developing a deep understanding of our own emotions, triggers, and coping patterns.

- o By increasing our self-awareness, we can catch ourselves in moments of stress and consciously choose how to respond.

- o Practices like journaling, therapy, and soliciting feedback from trusted others can help us build self-awareness.

3. Self-Care

- o Self-care refers to the practices and habits that nourish our physical, emotional, and mental well-being.

- o When we're well-rested, well-nourished, and engaged in activities that bring us joy and fulfillment, we're better equipped to handle life's challenges.

- o Building a robust self-care routine—one that includes healthy habits like exercise, good nutrition, sufficient sleep, and enjoyable hobbies—is a key component of emotional resilience.

4. Cognitive Reframing

- o Cognitive reframing involves learning to look at challenging situations from different perspectives.

- o Often, our initial interpretation of a stressor is not the only possible interpretation. By consciously reframing our thoughts, we can find new ways to understand and deal with difficulties.

- o Practices like thought challenging, looking for the silver lining, and asking "What can I learn from this?" can help us develop cognitive flexibility.

5. Social Connection

- o Social connection is a powerful buffer against stress and adversity.

- o When we have supportive, caring relationships, we feel less alone and more capable of coping with challenges.

- o Building and nurturing a strong social support network—one that includes family, friends, and communities of shared interest or identity—is a critical component of emotional resilience.

6. Meaning-Making

- o Meaning-making involves finding purpose and significance in our experiences, even the difficult ones.

- o When we can connect our challenges to our values, our growth, or our ability to help others, we build a sense of resilience.

- o Practices like reflective writing, engaging in creative pursuits, and volunteering or advocating for causes we care about can help us find meaning.

While these strategies provide a solid foundation for building emotional resilience, the real growth happens through consistent, daily practice. That's where resilience-building activities and challenges come in.

Here's a 30-day resilience-building challenge to get you started:

30-Day Emotional Resilience Challenge

Day 1–7: Mindful Mornings

- Start each morning with a 10-minute mindfulness practice. This could be seated meditation, mindful breathing, or a body scan.

- Throughout the day, take mindful pauses. Take a few deep breaths and observe your thoughts and feelings without judgment.

Day 8–14: Self-Awareness Check-Ins

- Set three alarms throughout the day: morning, afternoon, and evening. When the alarm goes off, check in with yourself. What emotions are you feeling? What thoughts are running through your mind?

- In the evening, journal about your check-ins. What patterns do you notice? How do your emotions influence your behavior?

Day 15–21: Self-Care Salon

- Each day, engage in one nourishing self-care activity. This could be taking a bath, going for a nature walk, engaging in a hobby, or preparing a healthy meal.

- At the end of the week, reflect on how prioritizing self-care impacted your emotional state and resilience.

Day 22–28: Cognitive Reframing Clinic

- Each day, identify one stressful or challenging situation. Write down your initial thoughts about the situation.

- Then, brainstorm three alternative ways of viewing the situation. What might you learn from this challenge? What strengths might you develop? What's one small positive aspect you can focus on?

- Practice adopting one of these alternative perspectives. Notice how it impacts your emotional response to the stressor.

Day 29–30: Meaning-Making Mission

- Reflect on a significant challenge you've faced in your life. Write about how this challenge has shaped you—your values, growth, and relationships.

- Consider how you might use your experience to help others. Could you share your story, volunteer for a related cause, or offer support to someone going through a similar struggle?

- Craft a personal mission statement that connects your life challenges to your sense of purpose and meaning.

Beyond this 30-day challenge, there are countless ways to integrate resilience-building practices into your daily life. The key is to find strategies that resonate with you and to commit to them consistently.

Here are a few more resilience-building exercises to try:

Exercise 1: Gratitude Journaling

1. Each day, write down three things you're grateful for. These can be big or small—from a supportive conversation with a friend to the warmth of the sun on your face.

2. Reflect on how focusing on gratitude impacts your overall emotional state and capacity to handle stress.

Exercise 2: Stress Inoculation Training

1. Identify a stressor you commonly face, such as public speaking, difficult conversations, or tight deadlines.

2. Visualize yourself handling this stressor with calm, confidence, and competence. What do you say to yourself? How do you breathe? What do you focus on?

3. Gradually expose yourself to this stressor in real life, starting with low-stakes situations and building up to more challenging ones. Practice applying the coping strategies you visualized.

4. Reflect on how this gradual exposure helps build your resilience muscle.

Exercise 3: Resilience Role Models

1. Identify three people—from your personal life, from history, or from public figures—who embody resilience.

2. Research their stories. What challenges did they face? How did they cope and thrive in the face of adversity?

3. Write about the lessons you can learn from their examples. How can you apply their strategies and mindsets to your own life?

Remember, building emotional resilience is a lifelong journey. There will be days when you feel strong and capable and others when you feel vulnerable and overwhelmed. This is normal and part of the human experience.

The goal is not to eliminate stress or adversity but to develop the tools and inner resources to meet these challenges with flexibility, self-compassion, and a growth mindset. Every challenge you face is an opportunity to strengthen your resilience muscle and prove to yourself that you can handle more than you thought possible.

Exercise 4: Resilience Anchors

Resilience anchors are practices, activities, or resources that provide a sense of grounding, stability, and support during times of stress.

Having a go-to set of resilience anchors can help you maintain emotional equilibrium and perspective when challenges arise.

1. Identify Your Anchors

    o   Reflect on the activities, practices, people, or places that make you feel grounded, centered, and resilient. Make a list of your top 5–10 resilience anchors. These might include:

        ▪   a meditation or yoga practice

        ▪   a favorite place in nature

        ▪   a creative hobby or outlet

        ▪   an inspiring book, song, or movie

        ▪   a comforting ritual or routine

        ▪   a supportive friend or family member

2. Create Anchor Cards

    o   For each resilience anchor, create a small card or note. On one side, write the name of the anchor. On the other side, write a few key words or phrases that describe how this anchor supports your resilience. For example: [Front] Walking in the Woods [Back] Grounding, Perspective, Peace. Keep your anchor cards in a place where you'll see them regularly: your wallet, your desk, your bathroom mirror.

3. Practice Dropping Anchor

    o   When you notice yourself feeling stressed, overwhelmed, or emotionally reactive, pause and "drop anchor." Choose one of your resilience anchor cards. Take a moment to connect with the words and feelings associated with that anchor. If possible, engage with that anchor directly. Take a walk in nature, call a supportive friend, or engage in a comforting ritual. If you can't engage with the anchor directly, visualize yourself doing so. Imagine the sights, sounds, smells, and sensations associated with that anchor. Breathe into the feelings of grounding and support.

4. Reflect and Refine

   o After practicing with your resilience anchors for a while, reflect on your experience. Which anchors were most effective at providing a sense of grounding and perspective? Are there any new anchors you'd like to add to your tool kit? Consider sharing your resilience anchors with a trusted friend or therapist. Invite them to share their own anchors with you.

As you commit to these resilience-building practices, be patient and kind with yourself. Celebrate every victory, no matter how small. And remember, you are not alone in this journey. Reach out for support when you need it, and offer your own hard-earned wisdom and compassion to others on the path.

With every challenge you face and overcome, you are not just building your own resilience but contributing to a more resilient world. Your courage and determination in the face of adversity ripples out, inspiring and uplifting those around you.

So, keep going, resilient one. Keep strengthening that inner core of strength, wisdom, and adaptability. Trust that you have within you all the resources you need to weather any storm and emerge even stronger on the other side.

Your resilient heart is a gift to the world. Never forget how powerful you are.

Part 4:

Integration and Freedom

Welcome to the final part of your inner child healing journey. In the previous sections, you've courageously faced and healed the wounds of your past, rewritten your inner narrative, and developed resilience to navigate life's challenges. Now, it's time to integrate all these transformative changes and step into a life of authentic freedom.

In this section, we'll explore how advances in neuroscience are validating and empowering the inner child healing process. You'll gain a simplified understanding of key neuroscientific concepts and how they directly support your healing journey.

We'll also delve into practical strategies for preventing the reinforcement of old emotional wounds. You'll learn how to create a prevention plan that encompasses conscious parenting, healthy relationships, and sustainable self-care practices.

A key focus of this section is the integration of your healed inner child into your adult self. Through powerful visualization and integration exercises, you'll learn to merge these two aspects of yourself, creating a unified, whole self that can navigate the world with confidence and joy.

To support your ongoing healing, we'll explore long-term strategies for maintaining emotional health. You'll receive a practical monthly checklist to keep you on track with your self-care and growth.

Finally, we'll celebrate the ultimate goal of this journey: living freely, unencumbered by the pain of the past. You'll be guided through creative exercises to express your authentic self and embrace your newfound freedom.

Get ready to experience the incredible rewards of your healing work. As you integrate your transformation and step into your freedom, you're not just changing your own life but contributing to a global shift toward greater emotional wellness and conscious living.

Advances in Neuroscience: Empowering Inner Child Healing

Welcome to this fascinating exploration of how advances in neuroscience are validating and empowering the inner child healing journey. In recent years, the field of neuroscience has made groundbreaking discoveries about the brain's capacity for change and healing. These insights provide a scientific foundation for the transformative practices you've been engaging in throughout this book.

At the heart of this neuroscientific understanding is the concept of neuroplasticity. Neuroplasticity refers to the brain's ability to reorganize itself by forming new neural connections throughout life. This means that our brains are not fixed and unchangeable, as was once believed but are dynamic and adaptable.

Why is this so important for inner child healing? Because it means that no matter what wounds we experienced in childhood, no matter how long we've been carrying patterns of thought and behavior, we have the capacity to rewire our brains for healing and wholeness.

When we experience trauma or adversity in childhood, it impacts the development of our brain. Chronic stress, for example, can lead to an overactive amygdala (the brain's fear center) and an underactive prefrontal cortex (the part of the brain responsible for emotional regulation and rational thinking). This can leave us more reactive to stress and less able to cope with challenges.

However, through practices like the ones you've been learning—self-awareness, self-compassion, reframing beliefs, and developing resilience—we can literally change the structure and function of our brains. We can strengthen the neural pathways associated with safety, calm, and connection and weaken those associated with fear, anxiety, and reactivity.

Another key neuroscientific concept is the power of experience-dependent neuroplasticity. This means that the brain changes in response to our experiences and environment. Every time we practice a new skill or engage in a new behavior, we are forming and strengthening neural connections.

In the context of inner child healing, this means that every time you practice self-love, choose a new, empowering belief, and respond to your emotions with compassion rather than judgment, you are literally rewiring your brain. You are creating a new default mode of being. One neuroscientific discovery that can profoundly support this process is the existence of mirror neurons.

Mirror Neuron Empathy Exercise

This exercise leverages the power of mirror neurons, a fascinating neuroscientific discovery, to deepen self-empathy and accelerate inner child healing.

Mirror neurons are a type of brain cell that respond equally when we perform an action and when we witness someone else performing the same action. They are thought to be the neural basis of empathy, allowing us to literally feel what others are feeling.

In this exercise, you'll be using mirror neurons to empathize with your inner child, strengthening the neural pathways of self-love and understanding.

Step 1: Preparing: Find a private space with a mirror where you won't be disturbed. Take a few deep breaths and ground yourself in the present moment. Remember a time when you felt deep empathy and understanding for another person. Notice how that felt in your body.

Step 2: Connecting With Your Inner Child: Look into the mirror and imagine your inner child looking back at you. Notice the expression on their face and the emotions in their eyes. Connect with their feelings. Are they scared, sad, lonely, or angry? Allow yourself to feel these emotions in your own body. Let your mirror neurons fire, creating a bridge of empathy between you and your inner child.

Step 3: Offering Empathy and Understanding: As you continue to look into the mirror, begin to offer your inner child words of empathy and understanding. You might say things like: "I can see how scared and alone you feel. It's okay to feel that way." "I understand your anger. You have every right to feel angry about what happened." "I feel your sadness. It's a valid and natural response to what you went through."

Allow your words to come from a place of deep empathy. Imagine them resonating in your inner child's being, just as they're resonating in your own body.

Step 4: Using Neuroplastic Visualization: As you continue to offer these words of empathy, visualize them creating new neural pathways in your brain. Imagine these pathways glowing and strengthening, forming a robust network of self-understanding and self-compassion. Visualize this network expanding, overwriting old pathways of self-judgment and self-criticism.

Step 5: Integrating and Reflecting: Take a deep breath and gently bring your awareness back to the present. Offer yourself a moment of gratitude for the empathy and understanding you've just cultivated.

Reflect on your experience. What did it feel like to empathize with your inner child in this way? What insights arose? Consider how you can continue to strengthen these pathways of self-empathy in your daily life, perhaps by practicing this exercise regularly or by catching moments of self-judgment and replacing them with understanding.

This process is enhanced by practices that integrate both mind and body. Neuroscience has shown that the brain doesn't distinguish between the physical and the emotional; it processes all experiences through the same neural pathways. This is why practices like yoga, mindfulness, and somatic therapy can be so powerful for healing trauma. They help us release stored emotional pain from the body and rewire the brain for greater integration and resilience.

Neuroscience also highlights the critical role of relationships in shaping the brain. Our earliest relationships with caregivers form the blueprint for our sense of safety, trust, and connection in the world. When these early relationships are characterized by attunement, responsiveness, and love, we develop a secure attachment style and a healthy sense of self.

However, when these early relationships are inconsistent, neglectful, or abusive, they can lead to insecure attachment styles and a host of emotional challenges. The good news is that through the power of neuroplasticity, we can rewire our attachment patterns. By cultivating safe, nurturing relationships—with therapists, friends, partners, and most importantly, with ourselves—we can develop what's called "earned secure attachment."

This is the essence of inner child work: becoming the loving, attuned parent to ourselves that we may not have had growing up. Every time we offer our inner child the presence, validation, and care they need, we are forming new neural pathways of secure attachment. We are rewiring our brains for love and belonging.

To help you experience this rewiring process firsthand, we've included a powerful exercise. This exercise combines visualization, self-compassion, and embodiment to help you strengthen the neural pathways of safety, connection, and love.

As you engage in this exercise, remember that your brain is incredibly resilient. No matter your age or life experiences, you have the capacity to change and heal. Every small step you take on this journey matters. Every moment of self-compassion, every reframed thought, and every boundary set is a victory for your healing.

Of course, rewiring the brain takes time and consistent practice. There will be days when your old neural pathways feel more familiar than your new ones. This is normal and expected. Healing is not a linear process but a spiral one; we revisit the same lessons at deeper and deeper levels.

The key is to keep showing up for yourself with patience and commitment. Trust that every loving action is making a difference, even if you can't see it yet. Over time, your new patterns of thought and behavior will feel more and more natural, more and more like home.

As you continue on this path of healing, let the insights of neuroscience be a source of validation and empowerment. You are not broken; you are wired for healing. Your brain is designed to learn, grow, and change throughout your lifetime. By harnessing the power of neuroplasticity, you are reclaiming your birthright to wholeness and joy.

So, keep going, brave one. Keep rewiring your brain for love and resilience. Keep becoming the most healed, whole version of yourself. The science is on your side, and so am I. I believe in the incredible capacity of your beautiful brain to heal and transform.

Exercise: Rewiring the Brain for Safety and Connection

This exercise is designed to help you strengthen the neural pathways associated with safety, connection, and self-love. It combines visualization, self-compassion, and embodiment to provide a powerful experience of rewiring your brain.

1. Create a Safe Space

   o Find a quiet, comfortable place where you won't be disturbed.

   o Make the space feel nurturing and safe. You might dim the lights, light a candle, wrap yourself in a soft blanket, or play soothing music.

   o Take a few deep breaths and allow yourself to settle into the present moment.

2. Connect With Your Inner Child

   o Close your eyes and imagine your inner child standing in front of you.

   o Notice how they look, how they're feeling. Are they scared, anxious, lonely?

- o Extend your arms and invite them into a gentle embrace. Let them know that you're here now and that you're going to keep them safe.

3. Offer Words of Compassion

   - o With your inner child still in your arms, begin to offer them words of love and reassurance.

   - o You might say things like:

     - ▪ "I'm here with you. You're safe now."

     - ▪ "I'm sorry you had to go through those hard things. It wasn't your fault."

     - ▪ "You are so brave, so strong. I'm proud of you."

     - ▪ "I love you unconditionally. You are worthy of love just as you are."

   - o Allow these words to flow from your heart. Trust that you know exactly what your inner child needs to hear.

4. Visualize the Rewiring

   - o As you continue to offer these words of love, begin to visualize them as golden light flowing from your heart into your inner child's body.

   - o Imagine this light forming new neural pathways in their brain—pathways of safety, trust, and belonging.

   - o See these new pathways glowing brighter and stronger with each word of love, each moment of connection.

5. Embody the Healing

   - o Now, imagine this golden light flowing back into your own body.

- o Feel it rewiring your own brain, strengthening your capacity for self-love and emotional resilience.

- o Notice how your body feels as these new pathways are formed. Is there a sense of warmth, of expansion, of lightness?

6. Integrate and Ground

- o When you feel ready, slowly open your eyes.

- o Take a moment to ground yourself in the present. Notice your surroundings and feel your body in contact with the ground.

- o Take a few deep breaths and offer yourself a moment of gratitude for the healing work you've just done.

7. Reflect and Journal

- o In your journal, write about your experience with this exercise.

- o What did you notice? What emotions came up? What felt most powerful or transformative?

- o Consider how you can continue to strengthen these new neural pathways in your daily life. What small acts of self-love and compassion can you practice?

Remember, rewiring the brain is a gradual process. Be patient and gentle with yourself as you engage in this work. Trust that every moment of self-connection, every word of kindness directed toward your inner child, is making a real and lasting difference.

You are rewiring your brain for greater wholeness, resilience, and joy. This is the power of neuroplasticity, and it is a power that is always available to you.

Your brain is healing with every loving thought. I believe in you and the incredible transformations you are creating, one neural pathway at a time.

Preventing the Reinforcement of Inner Wounds

Welcome to this essential chapter on preventing the reinforcement of inner wounds. As you've journeyed through the process of inner child healing, you've courageously faced and tended to the wounds of your past. You've learned to recognize, validate, and respond to your inner child's needs with love and compassion.

Now, as we move forward, it's crucial to explore how we can prevent these wounds from being perpetuated or reactivated in our current lives. This involves developing awareness of the subtle ways we might be reinforcing old patterns, as well as creating proactive strategies for parenting, relationships, and self-care.

One key way we can inadvertently reinforce inner wounds is through our inner dialogue. Even as we're working to heal, we may find ourselves slipping into old habits of self-criticism, self-doubt, or self-neglect. We might dismiss our needs, push ourselves too hard, or hold ourselves to unrealistic standards of perfection.

These patterns of self-talk are often deeply ingrained, echoes of the messages we received in childhood. However, as adults, we have the power to consciously shift this inner dialogue. Every time we catch ourselves in a moment of self-judgment or self-abandonment, we have an opportunity to choose a different response.

This might look like:

- replacing self-criticism with self-compassion

- meeting our own needs with the same dedication we offer others

- giving ourselves permission to rest, to make mistakes, to be human

- Celebrating our progress and efforts rather than fixating on outcomes

Another way we might reinforce inner wounds is through our relationships. We may find ourselves drawn to dynamics that recreate the emotional environment of our childhood—relationships where our needs are not met, our boundaries are not respected, or our worth is conditional.

While these patterns can feel familiar and even strangely comfortable, they ultimately prevent us from experiencing the healing power of healthy, nurturing connections. To break these cycles, we need to develop a keen awareness of our relational patterns and actively cultivate relationships that support our ongoing growth and healing.

This might involve:

- setting clear, compassionate boundaries in our interactions

- communicating our needs and emotions openly and assertively

- seeking out relationships with emotionally mature, supportive individuals

- being willing to let go of relationships that consistently drain or harm us

One powerful way to practice setting boundaries and advocating for your inner child's needs is through roleplay.

Inner Child Advocate Roleplay

This exercise is designed to help you practice advocating for your inner child's needs and setting healthy boundaries in challenging situations.

1. Imagine a scenario where your inner child might feel vulnerable, triggered, or unheard. This could be a conversation with a critical family member, a disagreement with a partner, or a stressful situation at work.

2. Write down the details of this scenario, including the setting, the people involved, and the specific words or actions that might be triggering for your inner child.

3. Now, imagine that you have the ability to press "pause" on this scenario. You can step in as your inner child's advocate, voicing their needs and setting clear boundaries. Write a script for how you would respond in this situation as your inner child's advocate. Consider:

   o What does your inner child need to feel safe and heard in this moment?

   o What boundaries need to be set to protect your inner child's emotional well-being?

   o How can you communicate these needs and boundaries clearly and assertively?

      ▪ For example: "When you criticize my choices, my inner child feels scared and ashamed. I need you to respect my decisions, even if you disagree with them."

      ▪ "My inner child is feeling overwhelmed right now and needs some quiet time alone to recharge. I'm going to take a break from this conversation, and we can revisit it when I'm feeling more grounded."

4. Practice delivering your script out loud. Notice how it feels in your body to advocate for your inner child's needs. Notice any resistance or discomfort that arises and meet it with compassion.

5. Reflect on how this roleplay might translate into real-life situations. What do you need to feel prepared and empowered to advocate for your inner child in the moment?

6. Consider creating some go-to phrases or affirmations that you can draw upon when your inner child needs support, such as: "I am here for you and will keep you safe." "Your needs are valid and important." "It's okay to take space or say no when something doesn't feel right."

In addition to our inner dialogue and relationships, our lifestyle choices and daily habits can also play a significant role in either reinforcing or healing inner wounds. When we're in survival mode, it's easy to neglect the basic practices that nurture our physical, emotional, and spiritual well-being.

However, consistent self-care is not a luxury but a necessity for preventing the reactivation of old wounds. By tending to our needs on a daily basis, we send a powerful message to our inner child: you matter, your needs are important, and you are worthy of love and care.

A holistic self-care practice might include:

- nourishing our bodies with healthy food, regular movement, and sufficient rest

- engaging in activities that bring us joy, relaxation, and creative expression

- cultivating mindfulness and self-awareness through practices like meditation or journaling

- seeking support when needed, whether through therapy, support groups, or trusted friends

To help you integrate these strategies into your life, we've included a Prevention Plan exercise on the next page. This exercise will guide you through the process of creating a personalized plan for parenting your inner child, cultivating healthy relationships, and practicing daily self-care.

As you create your plan, remember that prevention is an ongoing practice, not a one-time event. There will be days when old patterns resurface, self-care slips, or unhealthy dynamics creep into your relationships. This is a normal part of the healing process.

The key is to meet these moments with compassion and recommitment. Every day, every interaction, every choice is a new opportunity to align with your healing path, to choose love over fear, connection over isolation, nurturance over neglect.

As you continue to make these choices, you'll find your inner resilience growing stronger. The old wounds will have less and less power over your present reality. You'll be able to meet life's challenges with greater grace, groundedness, and self-trust.

Remember, healing is your birthright. By preventing the reinforcement of old wounds, you're not just protecting your inner child but claiming your inherent wholeness. You're creating a life that reflects your deepest values and truest self.

So, keep going, dear one. Keep choosing yourself, your healing, your joy. Keep parenting your inner child with the love and attunement they've always deserved. Keep building relationships and a life that honor your worth.

You are worth every effort, every boundary, and every act of self-love. Your healing journey is a gift not just to yourself but to everyone your life touches. As you prevent the cycles of wounding, you make way for cycles of love, resilience, and thriving to take root.

Prevention Plan Exercise

This exercise will guide you through the process of creating a personalized plan for preventing the reinforcement of inner wounds. You'll develop strategies for parenting your inner child, cultivating healthy relationships, and practicing daily self-care.

You'll need a journal and a quiet space where you can reflect and write without interruption. Give yourself permission to dream big and be radically honest about what you need to thrive.

Step 1: Parenting Your Inner Child

1. Reflect on your current inner dialogue. What are the common themes or patterns? Where might you be echoing old, critical messages?

2. For each negative pattern you identify, write a counterstatement—a loving, supportive message you can offer your inner child instead. For example:

   o Instead of "You're so lazy," try "You're working hard, and it's okay to rest."

   o Instead of "You're not good enough," try "You are inherently worthy and lovable."

3. Create a list of daily practices for nurturing your inner child. This might include:

   o setting aside playtime for activities you loved as a child

   o writing love notes or words of encouragement to your inner child

   o practicing self-compassion in moments of difficulty or mistake

4. Commit to one inner child nurturing practice you'll start implementing today. Set a reminder if needed.

Step 2: Cultivating Healthy Relationships

1. Reflect on your current relationships. Which ones feel supportive and nurturing? Which ones might be replicating old, unhealthy dynamics?

2. For the challenging relationships, identify the behaviors or patterns that trigger your inner wounds.

3. For each triggering behavior, identify a boundary or request you can make to support your emotional safety. For example:

   o If someone consistently criticizes you, you might request, "Please don't comment on my choices unless I ask for feedback."

   o If someone pressures you to overextend yourself, you might say, "I need to check my calendar before committing to anything."

4. Reflect on the qualities you want to cultivate in your relationships moving forward. What kind of people do you want to surround yourself with? What emotional environment do you want to create?

5. Identify one action you can take this week to nurture a healthy, supportive relationship in your life. This might be reaching out to a friend, setting a boundary, or expressing appreciation.

Step 3: Practicing Daily Self-Care

1. Reflect on your current self-care practices. What's working well? Where might there be gaps or inconsistencies?

2. Create a holistic self-care plan that includes practices for your physical, emotional, mental, and spiritual well-being. Consider areas like:

   o nutrition and hydration

   o movement and exercise

   o sleep and rest

   o stress management

   o creative expression

   o social connection

o mindfulness and self-reflection

3. For each area, identify at least one specific, actionable practice you can integrate into your daily or weekly routine. For example:

   o "I will drink eight glasses of water every day."

   o "I will take a 30-minute nature walk three times a week."

   o "I will journal for 15 minutes every morning."

4. Create a daily self-care checklist to help you track and prioritize these practices.

5. Identify any obstacles or resistance that might come up as you implement your self-care plan. How can you navigate these challenges with compassion and commitment?

Step 4: Reflection and Integration

1. Once you've completed your prevention plan, take a moment to reflect on the experience. What insights emerged for you? What feels most exciting or challenging about these new commitments?

2. Consider sharing your plan with a trusted friend, therapist, or support group. Inviting others to witness and support your intentions can be a powerful way to stay accountable and motivated.

Remember, your prevention plan is a living document. Be willing to adjust and adapt it as your needs and circumstances change. The goal is not perfection but consistent, loving attunement to your needs and growth.

As you implement your plan, be patient and compassionate with yourself. Celebrate every choice that aligns with your healing, no matter how small. Trust that every act of self-love, nurtured relationship, and tended wound is contributing to your lifelong resilience and flourishing.

You are doing sacred work. You are breaking cycles and creating new legacies. With every day and every breath, you are preventing the perpetuation of pain and making way for unimaginable possibilities.

Integrating the Inner Child

Throughout your healing journey, you've been cultivating a deep, loving relationship with your inner child. You've learned to recognize, validate, and respond to their needs with compassion and attunement.

Now, as we near the end of this journey, it's time to explore how to fully integrate this healed inner child into your daily life and sense of self. This integration is the culmination of your healing work—a sacred union of your past and present, your wounds, and your wisdom, vulnerability, and strength.

At its core, inner child integration is about embracing all parts of yourself with unconditional love and acceptance. It's about recognizing that your inner child is not a separate entity but a vital, cherished part of your whole being. When we integrate our inner child, we reclaim the joy, creativity, spontaneity, and wonder that are our birthright.

This integration also allows us to respond to life's challenges with greater wholeness and resilience. When our inner child feels safe, seen, and loved, we're less likely to react from a place of fear, defensiveness, or old trauma. Instead, we can meet the present moment with the full resources of our adult wisdom and our child-like openness.

So, what does inner child integration look like in practice? It's a continual, daily choice to honor and include your inner child in your life. This might look like:

- checking in with your inner child regularly, asking, "What do you need right now?" and honoring those needs as you would a cherished young one

- giving yourself permission to play, be silly, explore, and experiment without self-judgment

- bringing a sense of wonder and curiosity to your daily experiences and seeing the world through fresh, child-like eyes

- nurturing your creativity through art, music, dance, storytelling, or any form of self-expression that lights you up

- advocating for your inner child in your relationships, setting boundaries, and choosing connections that feel safe, respectful, and joyful

- comforting your inner child in moments of distress and offering the soothing words and loving touch they need to feel secure

One of the most powerful tools for inner child integration is visualization. By creating vivid, sensory-rich imaginings, we can provide corrective experiences for our inner child, rewiring old patterns and instilling new feelings of safety, love, and belonging.

Here is a visualization exercise to guide you in integrating your inner child:

Integration Visualization Exercise

1. Find a quiet, comfortable space where you won't be disturbed. Settle into a relaxed position, either seated or lying down.

2. Close your eyes and take a few deep, grounding breaths. With each exhalation, feel your body sinking deeper into relaxation.

3. Imagine yourself in a beautiful, tranquil setting in nature. This might be a lush forest, a serene beach, or a peaceful mountain meadow. Allow the details of this place to come alive in your senses.

4. As you explore this place, you notice your inner child in the distance. They're playing freely, joyfully, without any trace of fear or hesitation.

5. Approach your inner child with a warm, open heart. Notice how happy they are to see you. They run into your arms, and you embrace them with unconditional love and acceptance.

6. Hold your inner child close and whisper to them: "I'm here. I love you. I will always keep you safe." Feel these words resonating through every cell of your being.

7. Now, imagine a golden light emanating from your heart center, enveloping both you and your inner child. This light represents your adult wisdom, strength, and love.

8. As this light surrounds you, feel your inner child gently merging with your adult self. You are not losing or abandoning them; you are integrating their essence into your whole being.

9. Feel the qualities of your inner child—their joy, creativity, innocence, and resilience—flowing through you, fusing with your adult wisdom and life experience.

10. Take a moment to savor this feeling of wholeness, of deep self-love and acceptance. You are no longer divided or at war with yourself. You are one, whole, healed being.

11. When you feel ready, gently open your eyes. Take a few deep breaths and wiggle your fingers and toes, grounding back into the present moment.

12. In your journal, reflect on your experience. What did integration feel like for you? What qualities of your inner child do you want to more consciously embody in your daily life?

Another powerful way to integrate your inner child is through embodied play.

Embodied Inner Child Play

This exercise is designed to help you fully embody and express your inner child in a playful, physical way.

1. Find a private space where you can move freely without feeling self-conscious. This could be your living room with the curtains drawn, your bedroom, or even a quiet spot in nature.

2. Put on some music that makes you feel joyful, energized, and uninhibited. This could be your favorite childhood songs, upbeat dance tunes, or any music that sparks your inner child's delight.

3. Begin to move your body in whatever way feels good to you. Let your inner child lead the way; they might want to twirl, jump, shake, or just sway to the music. There's no right or wrong way to do this. The key is to let go of any adult self-judgment and allow yourself to be fully expressive.

4. As you move, imagine your inner child taking over your body. Feel the lightness, the joy, the freedom of being in a child's body, unencumbered by adult worries and inhibitions.

5. You might find yourself giggling, making silly faces, or even having a full-on solo dance party. Embrace it all! This is your time to let your inner child play and express themselves fully.

6. If any self-conscious thoughts arise, imagine them floating away like balloons. Keep bringing your focus back to the joy and aliveness of the present moment.

7. After you've danced and played to your heart's content, take a few deep breaths and check in with your body and emotions. How do you feel? What was it like to let your inner child take the lead?

8. In your journal, reflect on the experience. What did it feel like to fully embody your inner child? What insights or realizations arose? How can you bring more of this playful, embodied joy into your daily life?

9. Repeat this exercise whenever you feel disconnected from your inner child or just need a joyful energy boost. Over time, you'll find it easier and easier to tap into your inner child's embodied joy and playfulness.

Remember, inner child integration is an ongoing, lifelong practice. There will be moments when you feel disconnected or out of alignment. This is normal and okay. The key is to keep returning to self-love, to keep inviting your inner child into your heart and life.

As you continue this integration, you may find old patterns or behaviors naturally falling away. Things that once triggered or overwhelmed you may lose their charge. You may find yourself attracting people and experiences that reflect your inner wholeness and joy.

This is the gift of inner child integration—a life that is aligned with your truest, most authentic self. A life where your past and your present dance together in sacred harmony. A life where you embrace all of yourself with the deep, unwavering love you've always deserved.

So, keep going, dear one. Keep choosing integration; keep choosing wholeness. Your inner child is not a burden to be carried but a light to be celebrated. As you allow this light to shine through every aspect of your being, you reclaim the birthright of your joy, aliveness, and radiant authenticity.

You are a magnificent, whole, healed being. Your inner child and your adult self, hand in hand, heart to heart, creating a life beyond your wildest dreams. This is the promise and the power of integration.

I am so proud of you. I am so in awe of your journey. And I am so, so excited for the life that awaits you as you continue to embrace and embody all of who you are.

Maintaining Emotional Health

As we near the end of our journey together, it's important to recognize that healing is not a destination but a lifelong path. The work you've done to heal your inner child and integrate your whole self is not a one-time event; it's an ongoing commitment to your well-being and growth.

Just as our physical health requires regular maintenance—healthy eating, exercise, sleep, etc.—our emotional health thrives with consistent nurturing and attention. In this chapter, we'll explore long-term strategies to sustain your healing and create a monthly checklist to keep you anchored in self-love and self-care.

One of the foundational elements of maintaining emotional health is developing a strong self-care practice. Self-care is not selfish or indulgent; it is a necessary act of love and respect for yourself. It's about tending to your needs on all levels: physical, emotional, mental, and spiritual.

Your self-care practice might include:

1. Physical Care

   o nourishing your body with healthy, wholesome foods

   o getting regular exercise that you enjoy

   o prioritizing sufficient, quality sleep

   o taking breaks and resting when you need

2. Emotional Care

   o regularly checking in with your feelings

   o validating and expressing your emotions in healthy ways

   o surrounding yourself with supportive, loving relationships

   o setting and maintaining healthy boundaries

3. Mental Care

   o engaging in activities that stimulate and inspire your mind

   o practicing mindfulness and presence

   o challenging limiting beliefs and negative self-talk

o   continuously learning and growing

4. Spiritual Care

   o   connecting with your sense of purpose and meaning

   o   cultivating gratitude and awe

   o   engaging in practices that nourish your soul—
   meditation, prayer, time in nature, etc.

   o   expressing your creativity and passion

Remember, self-care looks different for everyone. What matters is that you're consistently making choices that honor and sustain your well-being. It's about listening to your body, heart, and intuition and responding with loving action.

Another critical aspect of maintaining emotional health is staying connected to your inner child. The relationship you've cultivated with your younger self is not something to be "completed" and then forgotten. Your inner child continues to need your love, attention, playfulness, and care.

Some ways to stay connected to your inner child include:

- having regular "check-ins," tuning into your inner child's feelings and needs

- making time for play and creativity

- writing letters of love and encouragement to your younger self

- advocating for your inner child in your relationships and life choices

- comforting your inner child in moments of distress or triggering

Keeping this connection alive ensures that your healing remains integrated and vibrant. You prevent old patterns of self-abandonment or self-neglect from creeping back in. You continue to parent yourself with the love, presence, and attunement you've always deserved.

In addition to self-care and inner child connection, maintaining emotional health involves developing resilience and adaptability. Life will always present challenges, changes, and unexpected turns. Sustainable well-being is not about avoiding these challenges but meeting them with flexibility, self-compassion, and a growth mindset.

Some strategies for building resilience include:

- practicing self-compassion, treating yourself with kindness and understanding in difficult moments

- cultivating a support system of people who uplift and encourage you

- focusing on what you can control, letting go of what you can't

- finding opportunities for learning and growth in adversity

- developing a sense of perspective, remembering that challenges are temporary and you have the strength to overcome them

As you integrate these strategies into your life, remember to be patient and gentle with yourself. Maintaining emotional health is a practice, not a perfection. There will be days when self-care slips, your inner child feels distant, and resilience feels hard to muster. This is all part of the human experience.

The key is to meet these moments with compassion rather than judgment. Remind yourself that every day, every moment, is a new opportunity to begin again and recommit to your healing and wholeness.

To support you in this ongoing commitment, we've created a monthly emotional health maintenance checklist. This checklist is designed to help you stay attuned to your needs, to track your progress, and to celebrate your ongoing growth.

Monthly Emotional Health Maintenance Checklist

1. Self-Care

   o I've been nourishing my body with healthy foods and sufficient water.

   o I've been getting regular physical activity that I enjoy.

   o I've been prioritizing sufficient, quality sleep.

   o I've been taking breaks and resting when I need to.

   o I've been engaging in activities that bring me joy and relaxation.

2. Emotional Awareness

   o I've been checking in with my emotions regularly.

   o I've been validating and expressing my feelings in healthy ways.

   o I've been surrounding myself with supportive, loving relationships.

   o I've been setting and maintaining healthy boundaries.

   o I've been practicing self-compassion in challenging moments.

3. Mental Well-Being

   o I've been engaging my mind in stimulating, inspiring activities.

   o I've been practicing mindfulness and presence.

o I've been challenging limiting beliefs and negative self-talk.

o I've been learning and growing in ways that are meaningful to me.

o I've been celebrating my progress and accomplishments.

4. Spiritual Connection

o I've been connecting with my sense of purpose and meaning.

o I've been cultivating gratitude and awe.

o I've been making time for spiritual practices that nourish me.

o I've been expressing my creativity and passion.

o I've been contributing to something larger than myself.

5. Inner Child Connection

o I've been checking in with my inner child's feelings and needs.

o I've been making time for play and creativity.

o I've been writing letters of love and encouragement to my younger self.

o I've been advocating for my inner child in my relationships and life choices.

o I've been comforting my inner child in moments of distress or triggering.

6. Resilience and Growth

    o   I've been practicing self-compassion in the face of challenges.

    o   I've been reaching out to my support system when I need help.

    o   I've been focusing on what I can control and letting go of what I can't.

    o   I've been looking for opportunities for learning and growth in adversity.

    o   I've been cultivating a sense of perspective and faith in my own strength.

At the end of each month, take some time to reflect on your checklist. Celebrate the areas where you've been consistent and compassionate with yourself. For the areas that need more attention, meet yourself with understanding rather than criticism. Remember, this is not about perfection but consistent, loving effort.

Another powerful tool for sustaining your emotional health commitment is creating an Emotional Health Vision Board.

Emotional Health Vision Board

Create a vision board that represents your ongoing commitment to your emotional well-being and inner child healing.

1. Gather materials:

    o   a large poster board or corkboard

    o   old magazines, printouts of online images, personal photos

    o   scissors, glue or tape, markers, etc.

2. Reflect on what emotional health and inner child connection look and feel like for you. What images, words, colors, and textures represent this state of being?

3. As you flip through the magazines and your own photos, cut out any images that resonate with this vision. Don't overthink it—trust your intuitive sense of what belongs on your board. You might include images that represent:

    o self-care activities that nourish you

    o relationships and environments that make you feel safe, seen, and loved

    o your inner child in states of joy, peace, and free self-expression

    o symbols of your strength, resilience, and growth

    o affirmations or quotes that inspire and empower you

    o your hopes and dreams for your ongoing healing journey

4. Arrange the images on your board in a way that feels balanced and inspiring to you. Use the markers to add any additional words, doodles, or decorations.

5. Place your completed vision board somewhere you'll see it often: your bedroom, your office, your living room. Let it serve as a daily reminder of your commitment to your healing, a visual anchor for the loving, thriving state of being you are continuously creating. Whenever you're feeling disconnected from your emotional health practices, spend a few minutes gazing at your vision board. Let it reignite your inspiration and resolve. Let it remind you of all the reasons your healing matters, of the beautiful life and world you're co-creating through your courage and care.

6. Consider updating your vision board as your emotional health journey evolves. Add new images and insights and remove

those that no longer resonate. Let it be a living reflection of your growth and transformation.

Remember, this vision of emotional health isn't a distant destination but a cherished companion on your life's journey. It walks beside you each day, inviting you to live and love with your whole, radiant, generously human heart.

Through this practice of externalizing and visualizing your commitment to your well-being, you deepen your devotion to the lifelong path of healing. You affirm that no matter what challenges and changes arise, you will continue to show up for yourself and your inner child with tenacious and tender love.

As you continue on this lifelong path of healing and growth, trust that you have within you all the wisdom, strength, and love you need. The practices and tools you've learned throughout this book are now a part of you, woven into the fabric of your being.

Draw on them often. Return to them with gentleness and grace. Let them support and sustain you as you navigate the beautiful, complex terrain of your life.

And always, always remember: Your commitment to your emotional health is a radical act of love—for yourself, for those who share your life, and for the world that needs your unique light. Every choice you make to prioritize your well-being, honor your inner child, and meet life with resilience and heart matters more than you can possibly know.

Living Freely

Welcome to this final and most joyous chapter of your inner child healing journey. Here, we celebrate the ultimate fruit of your labors—a life of authentic freedom, unburdened by the wounds of the past and radiant with the light of your true self.

Throughout this book, you've embarked on a profound expedition into the depths of your being. You've courageously faced the shadows of your early experiences, offering the tender, hurting parts of yourself the love and validation they've always craved. You've rewritten the narratives that once confined you, replacing them with stories of resilience, hope, and unbounded potential.

You've learned to nurture yourself with the gentleness and attentiveness of a devoted parent, advocate for your needs with clarity and conviction, and meet life's challenges with a grounded, resilient heart. Through this process, a remarkable alchemy has occurred—you've transmuted the lead of your past pains into the gold of a more whole, luminous, and free version of yourself.

This is what it means to live freely: to move through the world anchored in the unshakable knowing of your own worth, to engage with life from a place of open-hearted presence and authenticity, to dance to the rhythm of your own unique song without apology or hesitation.

Living freely is not about a life without challenges, for struggles and obstacles are a natural part of the human experience. Rather, it's about meeting these inevitable difficulties with a sense of grounded confidence and self-trust, knowing that you have the resources to cope, learn, and grow within you.

It's about no longer being unconsciously driven by the unresolved pain of your past, reacting to the present through the distorted lens of old wounds. Instead, you respond to life consciously and choicefully, informed by your history but not defined by it, guided by your values and hard-won wisdom.

Living freely is also about giving yourself unconditional permission to experience the full spectrum of life's joys and pleasures. It's about reclaiming the birthright of your creativity, playfulness, and innate capacity for wonder and delight.

For many of us, early experiences of trauma, neglect, or stress taught us to constrict our aliveness, view the world as a threatening place, or hold back our spontaneous self-expression. We learned to equate safety with smallness and survival with self-denial.

But as you've healed and integrated your inner child, you've gradually loosened these old bindings. You've remembered how to play, laugh, dance, sing, and create without self-consciousness or fear of judgment. You've reconnected with the boundless vitality and imagination that are your natural state.

Exercise: Gratitude Storytelling

1. Each evening, take a few minutes to reflect on your day and identify three moments or experiences you feel grateful for. These can be big or small, profound or silly.

2. Now, for each of these moments, craft a short, playful story, as if you were telling it to a cherished child. Use vibrant, descriptive language that captures the aliveness of the experience.

   o For example, instead of just noting, "I'm grateful for the delicious breakfast I ate," you might say, "This morning, my taste buds went on a wild adventure! They danced with the tangy sweetness of juicy raspberries, swam in the smooth creaminess of yogurt, and did backflips through the crunchy, nutty granola!"

3. As you tell these stories, let yourself embody the wonder and delight of your inner child. Allow your face and voice to be expressively animated. If you want, you can even illustrate your stories with simple, child-like drawings or collages. Don't worry about artistic skill - the focus is on free, uninhibited expression.

4. After you've finished your storytelling, take a moment to soak in the feelings of playfulness and appreciation. Notice how this practice shifts your energy and perspective.

This gratitude storytelling exercise serves multiple purposes. It trains your brain to scan for the good in your daily life, enhancing your overall sense of well-being and positivity. It gives you an opportunity to express yourself creatively without being self-conscious unselfconsciously. And it helps you connect with the enchantment and simple joys that your inner child so deeply craves.

As you make this a regular practice, you may find yourself moving through your days with a greater sense of aliveness, presence, and appreciation—all essential qualities of living freely.

In this chapter, we invite you to lean even more fully into this reclaimed creative freedom. We offer more guided activities to help you express yourself with abandon, unleash your unique magic onto the world, and revel in the sheer joy of being alive.

1. Morning Freewriting

   o Each morning, before engaging with the day's demands, take 10–15 minutes to free-write.

   o Put pen to paper or fingers to keyboard and let your thoughts and feelings flow without censorship or editing.

   o Don't worry about grammar, spelling, or making sense. The goal is to tap into your raw, unfiltered self-expression.

   o If you get stuck, keep your hand moving, even if you're just writing "I don't know what to write" over and over until new words come.

   o At the end, read over what you've written with a sense of curiosity and non-judgment. What themes or insights emerge?

2. Expressive Arts Exploration

  o Choose an art form that intrigues you: painting, drawing, collage, sculpture, dance, music, poetry, etc.

  o Set aside a dedicated time and space to engage with this art form freely and intuitively.

  o Let your inner child guide the process. Focus on the joy of creating rather than the end product.

  o If self-critical thoughts arise, gently thank them and return your attention to the sensory pleasures of the moment: the colors, the textures, the movements, the sounds.

  o When you're finished, reflect on how it felt to let yourself create so uninhibitedly. What did you learn about yourself?

3. Playful Adventure

  o Each week, plan a "playdate" with yourself where you embark on an adventure your inner child would love.

  o This could be exploring a new neighborhood, visiting a petting zoo, building sandcastles at the beach, or attending a comedy show—anything that sparks your sense of fun and curiosity.

  o As you engage in this activity, notice if any self-consciousness or "adulting" arises. Gently invite yourself to let it go and fully immerse in the child-like wonder of the moment.

  o Afterward, journal about your experience. How did it feel to prioritize play? What opened up for you?

4. Intuitive Movement

   o Create a playlist of songs that make you want to move your body with joyful abandon.

   o Find a private space where you can dance without inhibition. If it helps, close your eyes or dim the lights.

   o Press play and let your body move however it wants to. There's no right or wrong way to do this. The goal is to let your physical self express itself freely.

   o If thoughts of self-judgment arise, imagine them drifting away like clouds in the sky. Return your focus to the sensations of aliveness in your moving body.

   o After the final song, take a few deep breaths and check in with yourself. How do you feel? What did this liberated movement unlock within you?

5. Silly Storytime

   o Grab some children's storybooks from the library, or order some online.

   o Set aside an evening to read these stories aloud to your inner child.

   o As you read, let yourself fully embody the characters. Use funny voices, make dramatic facial expressions, and gesture wildly.

   o Let yourself laugh, gasp, and react with unrestrained emotion. Allow yourself to be completely swept up in the magic of the story.

   o Afterward, reflect on what it was like to let yourself be so expressive and uninhibited. What childhood memories or feelings did this activity evoke?

As you engage with these and other creative practices, you may find old patterns of self-doubt, perfectionism, or inhibition arising. This is normal. Remember, you're challenging deeply grooved neural pathways. Meet these patterns with compassion, but don't let them deter you. Each time you choose to express yourself freely despite these internal obstacles, you're reinforcing your brain's capacity for liberated, joyful living.

And this, dear friend, is the essence of living freely: continuously choosing to show up as your most authentic, unbridled self, no matter the external circumstances. It's a commitment to honoring your truth, your desires, and your unique expression, even and especially when it feels challenging.

It's a way of being that radiates outward, touching and inspiring all who cross your path. When you live freely, you give others permission to do the same. You become a walking testament to the transformative power of inner healing and self-love.

So, as you step forward into this new chapter of your life, let your creative freedom be your guiding light. Let your healed inner child be your constant companion, infusing your days with laughter, lightness, and impromptu dance parties. Let the unrestrained expression of your soul's magic be your highest priority and your greatest gift to the world.

And on those days when the old patterns feel strong, when the shadows of the past seem to loom large, remember this: You are no longer that wounded child, helpless and alone. You are a radiant being of love and light, forged in the fires of healing, imbued with the unshakable knowing of your own strength and worth.

You have within you all you need to meet any challenge, navigate any darkness, and rise again and again to the brilliant dawn of your own becoming. You are the living, breathing proof of the resilience of the human spirit, the indestructible power of self-love.

With every liberated laugh, uninhibited dance, and audacious work of self-creation, you are healing not just yourself but the world. You are contributing to the global uprising of consciousness and the unstoppable momentum of love and awakening, which is our collective birthright.

So, keep shining, dear one. Keep daring to live freely, to love fiercely, to create wildly. Keep embracing the total catastrophe of this beautiful, broken, hallowed life with the wide-open arms of your compassion.

The world needs your healed and untamed heart more than ever. We are all richer for your presence, courage, and commitment to the path of liberation.

If You Liked This Book, You Might Also Like...

Self-Love Revolution Workbook
Unlock Your Potential with Self-Compassion, Radical Acceptance, and Unshakeable Confidence

Minute Meditations for the Real World
Unlocking Peace and Productivity in Minutes a Day

Conclusion

As we come to the end of this transformative journey, I invite you to pause and reflect on the extraordinary distance you've traveled. From the first tentative steps of acknowledging your inner child's wounds to the courageous leaps of rewriting your story and embracing your untamed creativity, you have embarked on a hero's journey of the heart.

You have learned to listen to the whispers of your inner child, to offer them the loving attention and validation they've always craved. You have confronted the shadows of your past with the fierce compassion of a warrior, refusing to let them dictate your present any longer.

You have rewritten the narratives that once confined you, replacing stories of lack and limitation with empowering tales of resilience, potential, and worthiness. You have developed a toolkit of practices and perspectives to help you navigate life's inevitable challenges with grounded grace and flexibility.

You have reconnected with your innate capacity for joy, wonder, and unbridled self-expression. You have reclaimed the right to take up space, make noise, and dance to the beat of your own wild drum.

And through it all, you have discovered the most profound truth of all: that everything you've ever needed, every resource and solution and wellspring of love, has always resided within you. Your inner child, your inner healer, your inner wisdom—they have been your constant companions, guiding you home to the unshakable knowing of your own wholeness.

This is not to say that the journey has been easy. Healing is rarely a linear path, and there will undoubtedly be moments when old patterns resurface, when the shadows feel heavy, and when doubt and fear creep in. But these moments do not define you, and they do not negate the incredible progress you've made.

In fact, it is in these challenging times that your commitment to your healing journey shines most brightly. Each time you choose to meet your inner child's pain with presence and compassion, advocate for your needs and boundaries, and dare to express your authentic truth, you are reinforcing the neural pathways of resilience and self-love.

And each time you fall and pick yourself back up, dusting off your knees with a rueful grin, you are proving to yourself and to the world that you are unbreakable, that your spirit is irrepressible, that your commitment to your own flourishing is a force to be reckoned with.

As you continue on this lifelong path of growth and awakening, remember to celebrate every victory, no matter how small. Every self-loving thought, every act of courageous vulnerability, every belly laugh, and spontaneous shimmy are all testaments to your heroic heart and indomitable resilience.

And remember, too, that you do not walk this path alone. Every time you share your story, struggles, and triumphs, you are weaving yourself into the grand tapestry of human healing. You are reminding others that they, too, have the strength and power within them to transmute their pain into purpose, their wounds into wisdom.

In this way, your healing journey becomes a sacred act of service, a contribution to the collective awakening of our species. By doing the brave work of inner child recovery, you are not just changing your own life. You are participating in the healing of our shared world, one open heart at a time.

As you step forward into the next chapter of your adventure, let your healed heart be your compass. Let your reclaimed joy be your fuel. Let your hard-won wisdom be the lamp illuminating your path.

Trust that every step, no matter how faltering or uncertain, is taking you closer to the life of freedom and wholeness that is your birthright. Trust that your inner child is cheering you on every step of the way, marveling at the miracle of your becoming.

And trust that the universe itself is conspiring in your favor, aligning people, opportunities, and synchronicities to support your unfolding.

When you have the courage to heal yourself, life cannot help but rush in to assist you, bearing gifts beyond your wildest imaginings.

As our time together in these pages draws to a close, I want to leave you with the words that have become my anchor and my prayer:

May you trust the wisdom of your own becoming. May you embrace your inner child with the fierceness of a mother lion. May you speak your truth with the confidence of a thousand suns. May you dare to live and love and create with the audacity of a god. And may you know, beyond a shadow of a doubt, that you are worthy, you are whole, you are loved—exactly as you are.

With every fiber of my being, I believe in you and the unprecedented story you are here to write. Your healing journey has been an honor to witness and a blessing to behold.

And as you continue to walk this path of inner child recovery and radical self-love, know that I am with you in spirit, celebrating your every triumph and holding space for your every struggle.

The world needs your healed light. Your inner child needs your unwavering devotion. And your soul needs you to keep showing up with all your glorious imperfections and inimitable magic. As you step forward into this new chapter of integrated living, I invite you to continue sharing your light with the world. If this book has touched your heart, if it has supported you in any way on your path to wholeness, please consider leaving an honest review. Your words have the power to guide others to the healing they so deeply desire and deserve.

Know that I receive your feedback with the deepest gratitude and humility. It is an honor to witness your journey and to be even a small part of your blossoming. Your voice, your story, your truth—they are all precious gifts. Thank you for sharing them so bravely and beautifully.

As you continue to walk this path of healing, please remember that you are never alone. A whole community of compassionate souls is cheering you on, celebrating your every triumph, and holding you through every challenge. We are here for you, now and always.

And so, with a heart overflowing with love and gratitude, I bid you farewell for now. May you continue to tend to your inner child with the gentlest care. May you embrace all of yourself with the fiercest compassion. May you live each day as the miracle you are.

Until our paths cross again, dear one, keep shining.

Scan QR code to LEAVE A REVIEW

References

Blackshaw, H. (2020). *Inner Child*.

Bradshaw, J. (1990). *Home coming: Reclaiming and championing your inner child*. Piatkus.

Chopich, E. J., & Paul, M. (1993). *Healing your aloneness: Finding love and wholeness through your inner child*. Harper San Francisco.

Paul, M. (1992). *Inner bonding: Becoming a loving adult to your inner child*. HarperOne.

Taylor, C. L. (1991). *Inner child workbook - What to do with your past when it just won't go away*. Penguin Putnam Inc.

Made in the USA
Las Vegas, NV
23 December 2024

15242182R00085